Priscilla Lant.

Christmas 1947.

A LETTER FROM

GROSVENOR SQUARE

AN ACCOUNT OF A STEWARDSHIP

THE GUILDHALL PORTRAIT OF JOHN G. WINANT

Painted by James Gunn

A Letter from Grosvenor Square

AN ACCOUNT OF A STEWARDSHIP

BY

JOHN G. WINANT

LONDON

HODDER & STOUGHTON

FIRST PRINTED   1947

MADE AND PRINTED IN GREAT BRITAIN FOR
HODDER AND STOUGHTON LTD., LONDON, BY
HAZELL, WATSON AND VINEY, LTD., LONDON AND AYLESBURY

To
Geoffrey Story Smith

CONTENTS

vii

I

THE LETTER

Flat No. 30,
3, Grosvenor Square,
London, W.1.

Dear Geof,

To-day I am giving up my apartment in the Embassy building, and before leaving I wanted to take a last look at the rooms that were my lodgings for what seemed a very long time.

The late afternoon sun is casting a warm and friendly light through the windows. A gentle breeze is stirring the washed and worn curtains. The polished furniture, the scrubbed and waxed floor, give impersonal newness to the premises. The familiar objects of home and living are gone. To an outsider it would seem only a routine affair—a London flat being returned to its owners—but perhaps unusual here because, after five years of war, the inventory shows no damage except wear and tear, beyond a bit of shrapnel-shattered glass in one of the bedrooms. And yet, somehow, the simple act of closing the door for the last time grips my heart, for it means an ending of so much that has crowded life in the war years.

The flat has been my workshop and my living quarters. There are few men in British public life, whether in the government or in the armed forces, who have not stopped in at some time, and none in our High Command nor on special missions from the United States who has not made his way here, and many in the services have found here a night's lodging.

I

It is a practical kind of place with certain security advantages. It juts out from the main building with three outside walls, with the Embassy offices underneath and trusted people on the floor above. Here we prepared and received night messages. It was equipped with protected telephones, and from here we established a messenger service with Army and Navy Signals and with the Embassy code-room. The job called for twenty-four-hour duty and, although we arranged shifts for Embassy personnel, everybody worked overtime. In less than three minutes I could walk from the flat to my office in the Embassy. I never left either place in all those years without stating where I was going and how I could be instantly reached. It was because of the practical advantages of the flat that I decided not to live in the Ambassador's official residence which is a considerable distance away.

It was here that Constance joined me shortly after my arrival. It was here that General Eaker called us to say that our boy John was missing on a Fortress raid and where later I learned that he was a prisoner of war and held as a hostage. It was here that Tommy Hitchcock and I worked on the plans for the long-distance fighter plane, the P.51, and here that I was notified he had been killed on an experimental flight. These were personal things, but they meant much to me, and I know you will understand because you went to school with Tommy and John is your godson.

I loaned the flat to Mrs. Roosevelt when she made her visit to pay tribute to the women of Britain. It was after returning here late one night from the Foreign Office that I received a message from Washington announcing the death of President Roosevelt. It was here that I heard of the surrender of the German armies, of Churchill's defeat at the general election, and finally of the surrender of Japan. These are things that furnish and make a room, more than tables and chairs. Well, all that is over now, and I am moving to a small house down the street.

2

One of the deeper reasons for wanting to write to you is the growing disillusionment of to-day; which not only dims and obscures the present, but is trying to cloud the past.

It has seemed to me that many people do not understand the urgency of those days. Nor do I think it is sufficiently appreciated how much the British gave us in return for what we gave them, not only in loyalty and friendship, but in practical contributions.

You could not live in London in those early years and not realise how narrow was the margin of survival. It would have taken so few mistakes to bring about defeat; the miracle was how few were made and how unimportant in retrospect they were, although in war none is ever without importance, since all decisions touch life and death.

Constantly I was reminded of the old-fashioned hour-glass that was part of every kitchen in my childhood. When it was first turned for timing, the grains seemed to move slowly from the full upper bowl, but as the sands sank through the narrow vortex and the grains in the upper bowl lessened, how rapid was the descent! There were many times in the early years of the war when you felt the sands would run out and all would be over. If I say there were many times, at least four specific moments in 1940 and 1941 are fixed in my mind when destiny was to turn the hour-glass when only a few grains were left. In chronological order these four events were:

The Battle of Britain

Lend Lease

The German attack on Russia

The Japanese attack on Pearl Harbor.

The invasion of Russia and the attack on the United States were the great strategic blunders of the Axis powers. These decisions ignored the progress of science and the inexorable logic of the multiplication table.

One other factor came later that has recast the future for all men—

the invention and use of the atomic bomb; but the shadow of it was always there. The initial research on it was given to us by the British. The interchange of information began in the fall of 1941, and in the summer of 1942 we accepted the obligations of further development and manufacture. The British facilities were already overburdened. If we had not gone to war ourselves, it is very doubtful if we would have been willing to appropriate the huge sums of money and to allocate the necessary industrial facilities to produce this revolutionary weapon.

We know that the Germans had begun research in this field before the war, and although they were well behind us when allied victory came, it is only sense to realise that they would have organised its development if time had been on their side. But, as Mr. Churchill wrote in his statement on atomic energy after the destruction of Hiroshima, "By God's mercy British and American science outpaced all German efforts." The possession of this power by the Germans at any time might have altered the result of the war, and he added, " profound anxiety was felt by those who were informed."

They were well ahead of us, as it was, in developing radio-controlled rocket projectiles. If we had allowed other nations to go down before the invader one by one until we ourselves stood alone, we would have faced a militarised world organised against us. Can we believe, as we look back, that, had we remained neutral, we would have been sufficiently prepared in offense and defense to have sustained war under atomic attack in such a world?

It is true that there were many honest men at home who thought we were more effective in contributing the tools of war as neutrals than we would have been as belligerents. Yet when war came, after mobilising twelve million able-bodied men into the services, we tripled our production. Our slowness before we entered the war to take advantage of the war uses of radar in planes and submarines and to use the equipment the British offered us to protect our coastal shipping, and our failure to use our own installation at Pearl Harbor successfully, are added reasons for believing that all aid short of war was no guarantee of security.

In this same period when Great Britain held the line alone it was always possible that Japan would strike at Britain in the East. Faced at home with the threat of invasion, the British could not have found the forces to stop, or even seriously to delay, an advance which in default of armed American intervention might well have continued to the Persian Gulf. What effect such an advance might have had on German strategy and American policy in 1940–41 is a matter for conjecture, but the picture of Germany joining hands with Japan on the shores of the Indian Ocean, advancing through Spain and Gibraltar to Dakar, closing the Mediterranean, cutting off the Middle East oil, and severing Britain's life line to India and Australasia before the end of 1941 would not have been a pleasant one for us or for Russia.

It is because of these considerations that the fifteen months before we were precipitated into the war were, perhaps, the most critical of all. After the Battle of Britain the immediate threat of invasion passed; with the enactment of Lend Lease essential supplies were assured for those who remained on the battlefield against the Axis; the German attack on Russia massed land divisions to meet massed land divisions of the invader; the Japanese attack on Pearl Harbor made clear the combined purpose of the Axis powers towards the United States.

Not so many years ago we were rightly told that this was "a time for greatness." When I first read that phrase it made me think back to the days of Lincoln and of Lee, and I tried to sort out what really counted in the crisis that beset our own country when we were divided against ourselves. That, too, was a time for decision and a sense of *values, and called for sacrifice by the generous and the brave. I was sure if we could find the answer in our own past and in terms that were accepted by the people of the United States, the weight of the New World would be organised in support of those who were defending, in the Old World, our concepts of "life, liberty, and the pursuit of happiness."*

Always in times of stress it is the simple virtues that really count. In the welter and tragedy of the American Civil War, courage and kindness, common sense and a sense of humor, military competence and an abiding faith in the purpose of life gave strength and unity in advancing the dignity of man. These were the attributes that carried us through the First World War when we fought to defend democracy in the hope that the war we waged would end all war. Even in the disillusionment of facing another global conflict, we applied these same qualities of mind and heart to measure the issues involved and to sustain the national will after we had reached the decision to join with other allies to fight cruelty and aggression and to try once again to establish a lasting peace.

The war is over now. Often I have wanted to write you of the courage and the kindliness, the common sense and the bits of humor and the faith that I found in men and women here, but time and circumstance have not permitted. I have wanted to tell you the story of the war from the Embassy as I saw it, and so at long last I am sending you this letter from Grosvenor Square.

II

APPOINTMENT

IN January 1941 I received a telephone call from the White
House asking me to call on the President in Washington the
next day. I flew down from Montreal where I had moved
the International Labor Office from Geneva for the duration of
the war. When I went into the waiting-room of the Executive
Office "Pa" Watson greeted me in his friendly fashion, and
told me that the President planned to go down the Potomac
that afternoon to meet Lord Halifax who was coming in on
the *King George V*. He said with his usual genial laugh that
they had accused the President of wanting to get a look at His
Majesty's latest battleship. Five years later I was to sail the
Mediterranean on a battle cruiser with the President on his
return from Yalta and with "Pa"* on his last journey.

That day the President asked me many questions about the
men I had known in Europe during my long sojourn there and
about conditions as I had understood them in Europe and
Great Britain. There was a good deal to tell him. I had seen
sectors of the front from a plane while the battle of France
was raging. I left Paris the day before the Germans marched
in. I knew the tragedy of the refugee. I had talked with most of
the Allied statesmen of Western Europe. I saw the British
soldiers arriving in England from Dunkirk. I had seen the

---

* Major-General Watson, the President's Secretary, died on the
voyage home.

7

effects of aerial warfare over England. I was in the British
Foreign Office when Italy's entry into the war was declared,
and I was informed on the British military position and their
great need for equipment and supplies to carry on the war.
All these things we talked about. There was no mention of
the Court of St. James.

When I left him and went out into the ante-room, the
gentlemen of the Press asked me for a statement. I told them
I had nothing to say. It was not the last time I had to give
the same answer. I have always been grateful for their kindly
tolerance in not pressing for information which was not mine
to give. It was from the newspapers that I learned some days
afterwards, when I was back in Montreal, that the President
had sent my name to the Senate for appointment as Ambassador to Great Britain. I resigned from the International
Labor Office. Four days later my appointment was confirmed
by the Senate.

I had known the President for many years. Our early relationship had always been informal and friendly. He had asked me
to leave Geneva, where I was serving as Assistant Director of
the International Labor Office in 1935, to take the chairman-
ship of the Social Security Board. The Social Security Act had
just been passed in both Houses of Congress by enormous
majorities. It was considered a non-partisan measure and
therefore a non-partisan Board had been appointed to ad-
minister it. Its personnel was placed under the Civil Service by
statute. Although the President had named me Chairman, I was
the Republican minority member. In the summer of the 1936
campaign Mr. Landon repudiated the Social Security Act. I
believed in this legislation and was not only responsible for
administering the Act but had helped draft it. To my mind its

8

continuance became the most important issue in that campaign. I resigned as the Republican minority member of the Board and came out for Roosevelt for the Presidency.

When the campaign was over and President Roosevelt was re-elected, he told me that he wanted me in his Cabinet. I advised against it, for I did not think, since I had fought for what I believed to be a non-partisan measure, that I should then accept a party appointment. I did agree, however, to return to the Social Security Board for two months to finish the registration for old-age pensions, which had not been completed when I resigned.

Another reason that weighed very much with me was my belief that the Nazi and Fascist powers were determined on war. We did not belong to the League of Nations, and although I felt by that time that the League was no longer an effective instrument, I had hoped that, as we were members of the International Labor Organisation, we might still hold some influence over events. I also had a deep interest in its objectives, which were to raise standards of life and work to give a fairer chance to all people everywhere. I therefore decided to go back to the I.L.O. The President approved of my decision. Shortly after my return, I was elected its Director. This position gave me contacts with workers, employers and governments all over the world. The membership included more than fifty countries.

The Axis powers withdrew, one by one, from the I.L.O. The Germans had left in 1933 when Hitler came into power. The Italians denounced the League and broke with it over Abyssinia, but stayed on in the I.L.O. for a time. Their antagonism to the labor organisation, however, became obvious when the Fascist coalition tightened their collaboration during the period of their joint intervention in Spain. The Japanese followed the Italian pattern, but before they completely withdrew from the I.L.O. their contact with it was shifted from their Welfare Department to the Japanese Foreign Office. This indicated at the time closer collaboration with Germany and Italy on a common foreign-policy program.

Immediately before the attack on Poland by Germany we received through inadvertence a copy of the reorganisation of the German Social Insurance programs which had been keyed to meet war conditions. It is also interesting to note that the information on Mussolini's directive to stop all ships leaving Italian ports (which was issued just prior to the German surprise invasion of Poland) was first received outside of Italy by our Geneva office. Other evidence of unfriendly action by the Axis Powers was the planting of spies among the office personnel. They were interested in statistics on populations, industry and agriculture, and the division of employment. None of these statistics which were forwarded to the office by member countries was secret. All or any part of them could have been taken directly from the publications of the individual countries. It was, however, a convenience to find them centrally located and the analyses, compilations and the comparative studies undertaken by the Office were of use in measuring manpower and production in the respective countries.

While I was in Geneva I was constantly watched by the German and Italian secret police. I was also attacked in the German press. This conduct on the part of the Nazi and Fascist elements was not unusual in Europe at that time. I remember a disagreeable incident when travelling by train from Portugal to Switzerland. I was carrying a United States diplomatic passport. This was given me by order of the

President because my two predecessors who had served as Directors of the International Labor Office had been accorded similar courtesy by their governments when they were in the same position. It meant that by diplomatic custom and procedure an official's papers were not subject to search. When we reached the Spanish border a Franco customs official boarded the train to inspect the baggage and identification papers of the passengers. After this was completed we were ordered out of the train and directed to a customs office. It was usual to put the representatives of governments with diplomatic passports at the head of the list, but I noticed with what studied discourtesy I was kept waiting until the last passenger had been examined, and then rudely told I could get back on the train.

Just before crossing the frontier into France this examination was repeated. We were taken into a large, shabby room in which there was an office boarded off in one corner, and a triangular cubicle at the far end. The place was cold and barn-like and the men kept their hats on. Each passenger was taken into the office and roughly catechised by a miserable, egotistical bureaucrat. The moment the travellers passed through the office door I heard him shout to them to take their hats off. I did not want to be shouted at, or to be kept hat in hand while I went through this unpleasant ritual, so I put my hat in my bag. He was bright enough to understand and it made him very angry. He looked at my passport and then ordered two guards, who were standing back of him with rifles and bayonets, to take me down to the cubicle. I thought we would go through some more questioning, but when we got there and they closed the door, I woke up to the fact that they intended to search me. I refused to be searched, and kept repeating "No! Diplomatic passport!" They each stuck a bayonet against my stomach and, although I did not understand Spanish, I realised that I was being subjected to "pressure persuasion." The situation was awkward for me and apparently awkward for them. We stood in this odd position for about five minutes. Then one of them shook his head and said something to the other fellow, and we returned to the official. After an excited conversation among themselves, in which I felt that the guards were getting the worst of it, the official grabbed my passport, and, after looking at it again, made out the necessary papers. I gladly left Franco Spain and went across the border to what was then still free France.

My main preoccupation during these years was to make certain that the control of the organisation remained in the hands of the democratic countries, and that they were kept accurately informed on the European situation.

The I.L.O. was also active in combating Nazi and Fascist propaganda in the American hemisphere. When I first joined the organisation in 1935 I urged a series of American hemisphere conferences, which were later held. In November 1939, we had a meeting in Havana, Cuba, attended by the representatives of workers and employers as well as governments of the American nations, including the Dominion of Canada. A British observer attended on behalf of the British colonies in the Caribbean. This meeting, held after the outbreak of war, gave us an opportunity to offset the German-Italian effort to undermine workers' organisations in South America. The next year I visited South America at the invitation of the President of Peru. He asked me if I would go down to Lima and attend the opening of the hospital service and the pension system which were the results of simple beginnings by a

Peruvian expert whom I had assisted in working out the initial plans, and in which I had had a continuing concern. I agreed to do so provided the occasion would be used to bring together other American countries that were planning to carry forward similar social programs. It was at this meeting in Lima in December 1940 that we agreed on a plan for all-American cooperation in the field of social security.

My daughter, whom we call "Sis," wanted to help me on this mission. She was studying Spanish at the University of Peru in order to act as interpreter when I arrived. She had not been long in Lima when she wrote me she had met the German Ambassador to Peru at a party at the Argentine Embassy. He was directing a large sector of the underground German-Italian propaganda in that part of the world. He asked her many searching questions and I liked her reply. "You know," she said to him, "I am very young and frivolous, but my father is coming here in a few weeks—I suggest you ask him!"

On one of my journeys back to the United States from Geneva, at the end of 1938, some of those closest to the President urged that I tell him that he should again stand for re-election. I will always remember his cold anger when I told him that it was his duty to run for a third term. He answered very bluntly that he had done his part as a liberal and that some of the rest of us could share the burden of carrying forward the things we professed to believe. My appeal to him was that we were facing war; that he had a greater hold on the people of the democratic world than any other statesman of his time; that it was too late to find a substitute; that I understood his wanting to retire to Hyde Park to enjoy the freedom of private citizenship, but that I did not think that was good enough in the dangerous days that lay ahead. He looked wan and tired and it hurt me to say what I had to say. I asked him if he could not get away where he could be alone and think it out by himself. Then he made the only reference I ever heard him make to his illness and his handicap. He said:

"You know, Gil, I can never be alone." And pointing out of the window of the Executive Office, he added, "I cannot even go out and walk alone under those trees. Always someone has to be with me or near me. I am never alone."

I left the White House with confused emotions, and completely depressed, caring about him as I did, and understanding what "carrying on" must mean to him.

Later that afternoon I saw Ben Cohen, one of the most selfless people close to the President, and told him of this conversation. I will always remember his wise comment that "Events would make the decision for him."

Well, events did. But I understood what it meant to him when he said, sometime after his third inaugural, that no one any longer had a right to a personal life.

Much has been written about the President. I can understand both eulogy and criticism, but nothing that attacks the essential integrity of the man. If he played upon the meaner motives of others in order to win support, as some have said, whether for his own political advantage or for his country, I never saw it. It was foreign to everything that he ever said to me or that he did in regard to me, or the work he assigned to me, No one I have ever met was quicker to want to see good in the men I told him he could trust and rely on in the great crises that threatened the democratic world. I am certain that because I believed this I was able to help others trust and care for him. This does not mean that there were not differences of

14

opinion or that at times those in high command did not hold convictions that threw them into opposite camps both in relation to political decisions and to military strategy. But for all that, there was great integrity, absolute sincerity of purpose and devotion to a common cause.

When I last saw the President before leaving for London in February 1941 he outlined his conception of the task that lay ahead of me as Ambassador to Great Britain. He wanted me to keep Winston Churchill and the British Government patient while the American people assessed the issues which faced them. He further instructed me to make plain to the people of Great Britain that we believed in their cause, that Nazism and Fascism were incompatible with the American way of life, and he also reminded me, as I was leaving, that military training under the Selective Service Act had begun, American industry was keying to war production, Lend Lease was pending before Congress, and the transfer of fifty destroyers had already been accomplished. We had made our decision to do everything short of war.

From Washington I went to my home in Concord to accept an invitation from the Governor and the New Hampshire Legislature to address them before leaving the United States. I had served in both Houses and had been three times Governor, and it was an invitation which I deeply appreciated. It gave me a chance to talk directly to the people before taking up a new position in a foreign land, and I quote what I said since it shows in what mind I left for Great Britain in February 1941:

"A quarter of a century has gone by since I first served, as you are now serving, as a member of the General Court.

"Nothing is more real to me than the memory of those with whom I worked here.

"More than once I have told you that what we do alone is of little importance, because what we accomplish is always measured by what others can do in relation to it.

"There is nothing to-day in my opinion that means so much to this great country as unity in support of right action. Everybody counts. What we do together can never fail.

"It was here that I learned, in the years of depression, that the social and economic problems that we faced reached beyond state lines and across national frontiers. It was because I understood that, and because I realised that security, a stabilised economy and peace were essential to the happiness of all people everywhere, that whether in Washington or in Europe I felt that I was still working for you here at home.

"We know that the frontiers of democracy have been receding and the fundamental principles upon which this country rests have been challenged by those who would replace government by consent with government by force. I can illustrate what I mean quite plainly. Some days before the invasion of Czechoslovakia I visited Prague. Immediately following the invasion the students there protested, not differently than students might demonstrate here in America. Six students were shot by the invaders, the other undergraduates were placed in forced labor camps. The University was closed.

"For nearly five years now I have worked for an organisation in which there has been international representation by employers, by labor and by government. Many of the men with whom I have associated in the past have been killed or imprisoned, and the right to organise has been denied all workers in those countries which have been invaded.

"On the day Paris fell I drove across France to Geneva. I saw not hundreds, but thousands upon thousands of refugees; of farmer folk who had worked all their lives for what little they had and who had been driven out by the Germans. That is what happened to youth and that is what happened to workers and employers as well, and to their organisations. That is what happened to all people who came under the heel of the invader.

"And then there is another thing that I think we all realise to-day, and I think it cannot be said too often. The pillars of our Republic, the sinews of democracy, have to do with the right of free speech, the right peaceably to assemble, the right of a free press, habeas corpus, trial by jury and the right to worship according to our conscience.

"In the aggressor countries and in every country dominated by the aggressor countries, all these rights have been wiped out. There is no right of free speech, no right peaceably to assemble, no right of free press, and a denial of freedom of worship. All men are subject to arrest at will, without trial by ' twelve good men and true.'

"All those things that men have fought for here in this country, all those things that have made America what it is, are being destroyed in Europe.

"We are to-day 'the arsenal of democracy,' the service of supply against the aggressor nations. Great Britain has asked that we give them the tools that they may 'finish the job.' We can stand with them as free men in the comradeship of hard work, not asking but giving, with unity of purpose in defense of liberty under law, of government answerable to the people.

"In a just cause, and with God's good will, we can do no less."

III

ARRIVAL AND BASE-LEASE AGREEMENT

Just before I left for Great Britain Harry Hopkins returned to New York after having been sent to London on a special mission from the President to Mr. Churchill, the Prime Minister. We met at the Roosevelt Hotel. In the short time we had together he gave me a thumbnail sketch of the British statesmen and military and naval chiefs he had met on his journey and an extraordinarily accurate estimate of British civil and military needs. Immediately afterwards I took a plane for England. President Conant of Harvard University and Ben Cohen were on the plane with me. We stopped at Bermuda for fuelling and then flew direct to Lisbon where we changed planes, landing at Bristol. Due to a strong tail wind we arrived two hours before schedule. The committee of welcome had not arrived, so we stayed in the air over the landing field for an hour in a thunderstorm. The weather was very rough and this bit of the journey was not particularly enjoyed by any of us!

Just as the plane landed, the rain stopped and the sun came out. The Duke of Kent was there to represent the King, Brendan Bracken to represent the Prime Minister and the Cabinet, and Herschel Johnson, then Minister in London, was there from our Embassy.

We shook hands and the usual photographs were taken, then someone handed me a microphone and asked that I say a few words to the British people. I said what was really in my heart—that I was very glad to be there and that there was no place I would rather be at that time than England.

A special train was waiting for us, and on the journey the Duke of Kent explained to me that the King was coming to the station at Windsor to meet me, and that he and the Queen would be delighted to have me spend the night at the Castle, but that if I wanted to go on, the train would wait and take me to London that evening. I felt I should go to work as soon as possible and so declined the invitation to spend the night.

When the train stopped at Windsor station the King was standing directly in front of the carriage door. He took me up to the Castle in his car. The streets were crowded. With all my efforts at politeness I found myself sitting at the King's right, as I understood he had asked me to do. Remembering army regulations from the last war I was sure I was sitting in the wrong place, but I soon forgot this worry in the kindliness of my reception.

It was the first time in the history of Great Britain that a King had gone to meet an Ambassador. He was returning the courtesy which President Roosevelt had shown Lord Halifax, and I did not even have a battleship!

When we reached Windsor Castle I presented my letters of credence. We talked about his trip to America which he told me he and the Queen had thoroughly enjoyed. He spoke affectionately of the President and appreciated the message of greeting which I had carried to him. He remembered meeting me on a previous occasion and picked up a conversation where we had left off more than two years before. We talked about men in the government and the present state of the war. Then and always afterwards when I met him I found him to be completely informed on the day-to-day progress of the armed forces, and on any other subject that concerned his people. He understood my wanting to get to work and made my leaving easy. So I went on to London. When our train pulled in to Paddington Station an enemy air raid was in progress. Herschel Johnson and I had dinner and then went over to my office, so that I would have an opportunity of familiarising myself with the routine work of the Embassy.

When I reached my temporary rooms at Claridges that Saturday night I found a message from Mr. Churchill asking me to meet him the following Monday. Monday evening, however, Mr. Churchill was not well and I did not see him till the next night, when I had dinner alone with him.

I was happy to see at once that he understood the position of the United States and was appreciative of what we were doing. We spoke of the recent visits of Harry Hopkins and Wendell Willkie. Since Harry came as an emissary from the President to discuss specific matters on which the President wanted information and which were of mutual concern to the two countries, his trip had been largely confined to meeting with government officials. Willkie's visit was to meet the people of Great Britain. The fact that he came also immediately following his election campaign and had brought a letter from the President to the Prime Minister, together with his own genuine sympathy for the British cause, gave the besieged people of these islands a sense of unity in American support. The visits of these two men gave a tremendous lift to British morale within the government and among the people.

Harry had not intended to make a speech while in Britain, but Mr. Churchill told me of the few words he did say one night in Glasgow before his departure. It was at a small unofficial dinner at the station hotel, given by Mr. Tom Johnston, Secretary of State for Scotland. After Harry had spoken briefly, he turned to the group and said:

"I suppose you wish to know what I am going to say to President Roosevelt on my return. Well, I'm going to quote you one verse from that Book of Books in the truth of which Mr. Johnston's mother and my own Scottish mother were brought up: 'Whither thou goest, I will go, and where thou lodgest, I will lodge; thy people shall be my people, and thy God my God.'" Then he added very quietly, "Even to the end."

It was hard for Mr. Churchill to speak of this incident without being overcome with emotion. I got some sense of the strain of those early days when all an honest man could promise was "blood, sweat and tears."

He went on to tell of the President's letter that Willkie had handed him with its verse from Longfellow. You may remember it:

> ". . . Sail on, O Ship of State!
> Sail on, O Union strong and great!
> Humanity with all its fears,
> With all the hopes of future years,
> Is hanging breathless on thy fate!"

It was three months later when he gave public answer, and broke through his matchless prose into English verse:

"The last time I spoke to you," he said, "I quoted the lines of Longfellow which President Roosevelt had written out for me in his own hand. I have some other lines which are less well known, but which seem apt and appropriate to our fortunes to-night, and I believe they will be so judged wherever the English language is spoken or the flag of freedom flies:

> 'For while the tired waves, vainly breaking,
>   Seem here no painful inch to gain,
> Far back, through creeks and inlets making,
>   Comes silent, flooding in, the main.
>
> 'And not by eastern windows only,
>   When daylight comes, comes in the light;
> In front the sun climbs slow, how slowly,
>   But westward, look, the land is bright!"

During the days that followed I carried out a ritual which custom has sanctioned and I felt good sense would support. It meant calling on the Ministers of Government. I tried to turn these visits to good account by asking each Minister to describe to me the work for which he was responsible. The Prime Minister had told me, "You shall share our secrets," and other members of the Cabinet repeated this statement.

It is also encumbent upon a new Ambassador to call on all resident representatives of equal rank. Ministers call on the new Ambassador. Later the Ambassadors return the call. I used these formal visits not only to get acquainted with my colleagues but also to get as much information as I could from them about current conditions in their respective countries. We continued these exchanges of information throughout my stay here.

The transfer of the fifty United States destroyers in the previous September had been conditional on the British leasing bases to us in the Caribbean and on the American Continent.

A commission from the United States was in London when I arrived, negotiating these base-lease agreements. The members of the commission were Assistant Solicitor-General Charles Fahy, General Harry J. Maloney and Commander Harold Bessemeier, assisted by Theodore Achilles, a Foreign Service officer in the Embassy. The Commander was ill during the early part of the negotiations so that the brunt of the work fell on the two other members of the commission and Achilles, who together showed great skill and persistence in putting forward the American requirements. These negotiations had been delayed and complicated by colonial and dominion officials who had come on to London and had raised objections to what we thought were necessary concessions to secure the bases. We felt that sufficient recognition was not being given to the overall defense needs of either Great Britain or the United States. In granting self-government to some of the territories under the Colonial Office, the British had surrendered part of their authority to force action on Empire defense measures.

Since I was informed by the members of the commission that the negotiations had reached an impasse, I took the matter up directly with Mr. Churchill. He arranged a meeting the following morning for Herschel Johnson and myself, with Lord Cranborne, the Dominions Secretary, and Lord Moyne, the new Colonial Secretary. I explained that I was there not to negotiate but to expedite a conclusion of the negotiations and to emphasise the wider implications involved. Mr. Churchill himself that same afternoon met the American commission with Lord Moyne and Lord Cranborne sitting in, in order to narrow the area of disagreement.

I attended the meeting which was held at No. 10, Downing Street, normally the home of the Prime Ministers of Britain.

The door of No. 10 is probably as well known as the façade of the White House. The sight of either of them in newsreels or in pictures awakens in most of our peoples an affection and a certain proprietorship. They belong to the people—because the person who lives in them is there by consent of the people. For this reason there is never anything personal about these houses, for they do not belong to one man, they belong to history.

The Cabinet Room at No. 10, Downing Street is a long rectangular room almost filled by a massive table covered with green felt and surrounded by chairs. The table is laid with white blotter pads, paper and pencils, all neatly arranged upon it. The simplicity of the room is impressive. High windows look out on a small walled garden that is adjacent to the Horse Guards Parade. Double doors at one end of the room lead into the office of the secretaries. At the opposite end a door leads into the garden. There are two other doors, one into a small ante-room and one which is the general entrance.

I could not help but think of the history that had been made there and of the desperate pressures of the moment. Perhaps no men of any cabinet had been so sorely beset with difficulties as those who made up the Coalition Cabinet in that winter of '41.

The Prime Minister usually sat half-way down the table with his back to the fireplace, facing the garden windows, but on this particular afternoon he had moved to the far end where we sat together with the British Representatives on his side of the table and the United States Commission on my side.

I had never seen Mr. Churchill at work before, and I was deeply impressed not only with his grasp of the values involved and his appreciation of the defense needs of the United

States, but also with his knowledge of the detail of the negotiations with which he had familiarised himself on such short notice. I became quickly conscious of his vast experience in public matters which he had acquired during more than forty years of active participation in public life. I realised his advantage in discussing this problem in having served in the past as First Lord of the Admiralty, Secretary of State for War, Secretary of State for Air, Minister of Munitions in the last war and Secretary of State for the Colonies. He had also held in previous governments the office of Chancellor of the Exchequer, President of the Board of Trade, Home Secretary, and Chancellor of the Duchy of Lancaster, which ranks as a Ministry without Portfolio. There was no detail of the problem before us which was not alive to him and on which his knowledge of the past did not throw light as well as constructive criticism.

He visualised every type of attack that might concern the armed forces of the United States in defense of our Atlantic shoreline, whether by submarine or raider or aerial bombardment. He stated the problem of fuelling in all these types of operations. He showed extraordinary knowledge of the structure of the Empire and of the legal obligations involved in treating with the dominions and with the colonies. He had a lively and imaginative grasp of American public opinion in relation to the base-lease issue. In less than five minutes he had swept away as immaterial three-quarters of the objections which had been raised by his negotiators, but at the same time he questioned the military clauses which, because of General Maloney's skilful insistence, had been agreed upon.

One of the British legal advisers raised an obscure question of constitutional law which angered him as a theoretical and irrelevant legal argument. We remained seated but he left his chair and walked up and down the length of the room, muttering to himself.

He interested me intensely as a man, this stocky figure, with a slight stoop, striding up and down, suddenly completely unconscious of any presence beyond his own thoughts—a power of concentration I was to see repeated many times in many circumstances. He knew his country was battling for self-preservation. Yet in spite of the pressures I felt him to be a friend who, in accepting assistance, recognised it involved counter-obligations that must be fully honored.

After this conference, with further concessions by Mr. Churchill on the defense section, I cabled the President that the "former naval person"* had over-ruled the opinion of his advisers in order to meet our wants. I added that I hoped the new draft would be acceptable. The President replied confirming the action taken and asked me to convey his appreciation to the Prime Minister. This was one of the many occasions when knowledge and a sureness of purpose allowed these two men to reach a final decision on the shortest line of communication with the least waste of time. Each knew that prompt and generous action had its own reward.

On March 27th I was authorised to sign the base-lease agreement. Mr. Churchill signed for Great Britain.

* "Former Naval Person." This was President Roosevelt's way o addressing Winston Churchill in his exchange of messages after Mr. Churchill had become Prime Minister and before Pearl Harbor. Mr. Chamberlain had arranged at the beginning of hostilities to keep the President informed on the war situation. He delegated this task to Mr. Churchill who was then First Lord of the Admiralty. Since these communications were not part of a formalised procedure they were signed "Naval Person." When Mr. Churchill became Prime Minister the President addressed his replies to "the former Naval Person." After Pearl Harbor the exchange of messages was on a direct and official basis, although this method of address continued to appear in informal messages.

I appreciated Secretary Hull's later remark when there was a suggestion of changing this treaty contract to which we had agreed. He said that this question might be "more appropriately taken up by our great-grandchildren."

It is customary in Great Britain that the American Ambassador's first public address be made at a dinner given by The Pilgrims. This Society was organised by men on both sides of the water who felt that good relations between Great Britain and the United States were in the interests of world peace. Lord Roberts, the great Field-Marshal, was its first President in Great Britain. In the war years Lord Derby headed the British chapter and Nicholas Murray Butler was President in the United States. The last meeting of The Pilgrims had been at the time of Lord Halifax's departure when he left London on his journey to the United States to take over the Ambassadorship. In spite of his foreign post, Lord Halifax still continued to be a member of the War Cabinet. I would like to say that his courtesy and his friendship to me personally made my assignment to London easier in the long years in which we served in each other's country.

On this occasion it was decided to have a luncheon meeting because it was simpler in a time of austerity and also because of the black-out and the night bombing.

All members of the Cabinet were present, the proprietors of the British Press and other ranking men in British public life. Lord Derby, sportsman, statesman, man of affairs and a beloved character in all walks of life, left a sickbed to preside. Mr. Churchill was speaking for Great Britain. I was to speak for the United States.

Mr. Churchill in his address said publicly much that he had told me privately and ended by turning to me and saying:

"Mr. Ambassador, you share our purpose, you will share our dangers, you will share our anxieties, you shall share our secrets, and the day will come when the British Empire and the United States will share together the solemn but splendid duties which are the crown of victory."

In the stern realities of the aftermath of war, I believe that pledge still holds for the British people and, whatever storm winds blow, we can count on an ally who knows our way of life because it is their own, and, like ourselves, will die to defend it.

IV

THE BATTLE OF BRITAIN
AND BOMBINGS

I HAD been in England during the Battle of Britain. There is a story from the *Sunday Times* which presents in dramatic form the last phase of this struggle for supremacy in the air.

Mr. Churchill had gone to Uxbridge to the headquarters of Air Vice-Marshal Park who was in command of the fighter squadrons. On the great table in the operations room he watched the movement of the colored discs representing the advance of successive waves of German bombers. As each wave approached, Park gave his orders to put in more British fighter squadrons. The Air Vice-Marshal was calm and businesslike. Mr. Churchill was strangely quiet.

Each attack was successfully repelled, but to the waves of bombers there seemed no end. At last, unable to control himself, Mr. Churchill turned to Park. "How many more have you got?" he asked. Quietly, the Air Vice-Marshal replied, "I am putting in my last."

Their eyes fixed on the table, the two men waited for the next German wave. It never came. The Germans, too, had put in *their* last.

With tears in his eyes Churchill got into his car. It was on the journey back that the General Staff Officer with him heard him mutter to himself that forever-remembered tribute "Never in the field of human conflict was so much owed by so many to so few"—words that he spoke a few days later in the House of Commons and that were heard around the world.

Across the ocean the people of the New World understood the sacrifice of this gallant band who had died to keep men free and passed "through hardship to the stars."

These are things that move men and make history, but in modern war organisation and science also count.

It was faith in an independent Royal Air Force, whose commander and staff had learned from their first Air-Marshal, Hugh Montague Trenchard, the fundamentals of war in the air, that gave Britain the means for the "few" to defend the "many" and save England from invasion. The eight-gun Spitfire and Hurricane combat planes backed by radar detection and ground control were part of that defense.

In the summer of 1914 Trenchard was a Major in charge of two squadrons. They represented the Royal Flying Corps, the British Army air force of that time. Four years later he was the Commander-in-Chief of the Allied striking force (British, French and American) against Germany. The next decade saw the greatest work of his life; the rebuilding of the Royal Air Force from its foundations after total demobilisation, and the faithful defense of its integrity, its autonomy and its fundamental doctrine against the many dangers that beset its early years. It was to him above all others that Britain owed the airforce organisation that stood the supreme test in 1940.

Brigadier-General William Mitchell tried to do as much for us after the last war. He was court-martialled for his efforts.* We ourselves have reason to be deeply grateful to General

* Since this was written the United States has established, under the National Security Act of 1947, a Defense Department with a Secretary for Defense, and Under-Secretaries for War, Navy, and Air.

Marshall in the Second World War for his broadminded understanding of the needs of the air and his cooperation with and support of General Arnold, which was later reflected with equal generosity in the relationship between General Eisenhower and General Spaatz in the European area.

But if the R.A.F. had not been a separate and autonomous service it is more than doubtful that they would have been permitted (1) to get sufficient appropriations, or (2) to command the necessary manpower or, most important of all, (3) to build a force designed for war in the air and not merely for helping the Army and Navy win battles on land and sea. These three factors were essential in developing the superior combat planes with their heavier fire power, and the radar with its large ground forces, and in carrying forward the intricate, complicated scientific research that is necessary to maintain air superiority. The Navy would have wanted more ships with thicker skins and with more guns, and the Army, with its depleted land forces, would have hesitated to permit recruitments in sufficient numbers to man ground control efficiently. Each would have subordinated its air arm to its traditional tactics and strategy. The best example of starving a new arm of an old service is, perhaps, illustrated by the fact that the British, after inventing the tank in 1918, went into the present war without a single armored division.

It was the application of radar control to air warfare that made it possible to pick up the enemy planes as they left their airfields, and that enabled British ground control to place their defense squadrons in a position to intercept the enemy invaders. A hundred fighters with radar direction are more effective than a thousand without. This meant that the R.A.F. had, under its own control, communications which even extended to warning British areas of bombing attack. When war came to us I worked very hard to integrate our air arm with established British radar communication. This was accomplished. It saved many lives.

In this desperate hour for Britain a quiet figure held command. Air Chief Marshal Sir Hugh Dowding was responsible for the air defense over the British Isles. The French in their last agony of collapse had asked for more fighting squadrons and the British Cabinet was anxious to do everything possible to help them. Dowding was generous in wanting to give aid but he had measured with extraordinary precision the fighting squadrons necessary to defend Great Britain, and was adamant about ceding a single plane that would obliterate the chance of a free Britain in a future world.

I was glad, when Dowding came to the United States to advise us on fighter aircraft, to arrange a meeting with President Roosevelt, who saw to it that Dowding's knowledge and experience in fighter aircraft were built into our own combat airplane program. No greater honor was done me while I was in Britain than when the few of those "few" that were left gave a dinner to Dowding and asked me to be their guest.

The invasion of Britain had been planned to commence in the September of 1940. The following is an extract from a directive given by Hitler on July 16th, 1940: *

"Since England, in spite of her militarily hopeless situation, shows no sign of coming to terms, I have decided to prepare a landing operation against England, and, if necessary, to carry it out . . . The preparations for the entire operation must be completed by mid-August."

On September 7th, 1940, the British Chiefs of Staff con-

---

* House of Commons Debates, November 18, 1946.

sidered a report on possible German action against the United Kingdom. The main features of this report were:

"(a) The westerly and southerly movement of barges and small ships to ports between Ostend and Le Havre suggested a very early date for invasion, since such small craft would not be moved unnecessarily early to ports so much exposed to bombing attacks.

"(b) The striking strength of the German Air Force disposed between Amsterdam and Brest had been increased by the transfer of 160 long-range bomber aircraft from Norway; and short-range dive-bomber units had been re-deployed to forward aerodromes in the Pas de Calais area, presumably in preparation for employment against this country.

"(c) Four Germans captured on landing from a rowing boat on the south-east coast had confessed to being spies, and had said they were to be ready at any time during the next fortnight to report the movement of British reserve formations in the area Oxford-Ipswich-London-Reading.

"(d) Moon and tide conditions during the period September 8-10 were most favourable for a seaborne invasion on the south-east coast."

This report indicated that German preparations for invasion were so advanced that it could be attempted at any time. Taking into account the German air attacks, which were at that time concentrated against aerodromes and aircraft factories, the British Chiefs of Staff agreed that the possibility of invasion had become imminent, and that the defense forces should stand by at immediate notice.

The Luftwaffe had been given the double assignment of first destroying the R.A.F. and then preventing the British Navy from attacking the German landing forces.

A small group of American observers was sent by the President to Great Britain in the summer of 1940, and it has always been interesting to me that they could have evaluated so accurately the chances of the invasion.

The President was very conscious of the munitions and equipment that we had sent to the Continent which, after the capitulation of France, fell into the hands of the Axis. He wanted to make certain that this would not occur again in Britain, and that whatever was sent into this combat area, whether by private contract or otherwise, would be effectively used against those who had already belittled and who would betray our way of life.

It was for this reason that he sent Colonel, later General, Donovan, Major-General Strong and the then Lt.-Colonel Spaatz, with others to measure British military resistance. He asked me to go to England in order to give him my opinion on the morale of the civil population. Colonel Donovan's mission was related to the decision on the transfer of the fifty destroyers. General Strong reported on the determination of the Navy and Army to meet invasion.

The most constructive estimate on invasion, in my opinion, was made by Lt.-Colonel Spaatz. No man in the United States had a more accurate evaluation of the strength of the German air force than Spaatz. After talking with British pilots and personally inspecting and flying the latest British fighter planes he came to the conclusion that in spite of inferiority in numbers the British were in a position to maintain air supremacy over the islands and the Channel. He went on from this conclusion to say that against British naval strength the Germans would not attempt invasion. It was a close decision. The Germans had assumed that the British would not dare to subject their people

34

to a continual bombing and they would waste their fighting forces in resisting bombardments. This was not done. The British showed great restraint and frugality in the use of their fighter planes. My report to the President that they would take bombing, whether in the dock areas of the Thamesside or the Clydeside or anywhere else in the country, proved to be more than correct.

When the war was over General Spaatz's modest report on his meeting with General Donovan was a credit to both men. He explained that Colonel Donovan, after making a tour of Great Britain in August 1940, called a meeting of the army air force observers, namely himself, Lt.-Colonel "Monk" Hunter, Major McDonald and Captain Kelsey, and also a number of resident naval and army observers. The story goes that the naval and army observers, when asked what they thought of the British chance of survival, replied they had not got a hope. Lt.-Colonel Spaatz, on the other hand, said that he and the army air force observers were convinced that the British would pull through because the Germans could not beat the R.A.F. and they would not invade until they had. Colonel Donovan went back to the United States and reported these observations, recommending the transfer of the destroyers to Great Britain.

General Pershing helped prepare the American people for this action when he said in a broadcast address from Washington on August 4th, 1940: "Grave danger for us lurks in the present world situation . . ." and "It is not hysterical to insist that democracy and liberty are threatened. . . . By sending help to the British we can still hope with confidence to keep the war on the other side of the Atlantic Ocean." He urged that the fifty over-age destroyers be made immediately available to the British and Canadian Governments.

Two days later I was asked to speak on a national hook-up from Washington on the fifth anniversary of the passage of the Social Security Act. It gave me an opportunity to support General Pershing's statements:

"In building national morale, in protecting family income, and in matching men and jobs, the social security system has given to America a sounder foundation upon which to build its defense efforts than has been possible in any previous crisis. There is a larger security, however, which we must consider to-day. Having been in Europe for the last two years I have seen something of this war. I realise that the strength of America lies in the people themselves. Therefore we must solve the problem of our own defense. We have seen one country after another seeking peace, destroyed by war. I was in contact with those countries. I believe that the failure to act more promptly or in concert for their own protection was in large measure due to misplaced good-will and guilelessness. People were too decent to believe that after the experiences of the last war there were those who would, in fact, force a new war. I don't want that to happen here. I don't want to see us divided or unaware.

"The other day General Pershing spoke to the nation: I know, as any other man who has been in the service knows, that he has lived his life for his country and the soldiers who once followed him. I believe no more truthful warning has been made to the people of this country than his statement of August 4th. It is simply a fact that 'all things we hold most dear are gravely threatened.' Once more the guardians of democracy must go armed and alert."

It was not until six months later that I went to England to take up my appointment. It was a very changed country from the earlier days of the war. Everywhere the enemy bombing had left great gashes in the buildings of London, its suburbs and in coastal towns. Anti-aircraft guns were placed at all strategic points in streets, in parks, and in the countryside; and over London and southern towns hung a curtain of blimps to prevent low dive-bombing.

The pattern of civilian life had severely changed too. There had been a hardening of resolution and there was a sense of grim determination everywhere, which had been intensified after the fall of France and the heavy bombing which had commenced that autumn. The enemy raids had taken their toll o death, and it was a strange existence that people led in those days. When we think of civilian bombing in London we think of people taking cover in the public shelters and in the subways, but we often overlook the fact that the majority of people still lived in their own homes. In the larger houses people took shelter in a basement room or cellar, but in the smaller and less stoutly built houses people adjusted their lives to stranger conditions. Many people spent their nights in Anderson shelters, which were corrugated iron arches, planted deep into the earth and covered with soil. I have seen suburbs where almost every small house had one of these erected in the garden, and many thousands of people owed their lives to them. Families took up their nightly residence there, and in the damp and dark atmosphere, often with their neighbors sharing with them, spent uneasy nights sleeping as best they could amid the noise of dropping bombs and the whine of the anti-aircraft shells.

Later the Morrison shelter was introduced. This was a house shelter, table-shaped and made of steel, with a heavy wire netting around the sides to protect the occupants against flying objects and against falling ceilings. Families would huddle underneath at night-time and during the day the shelter would be used as a household table.

The stairway was usually the last bit of home structure that collapsed when a house was bombed, so that many a family relied for their night's safety on the closet under the stairway. Mattresses would be all the furniture the space in the closet provided for the communal dormitory. It was not a comfortable existence and there were constant hazards in areas where there were power plants and factories and dockyards, and in towns where the Germans began "Baedeker" raids on historic landmarks. Those unwilling to take a chance in their homes went to the brick shelters in the streets or to the subways. The shelters were constructed to withstand blast at close range. At night-time there would be a general exodus of family groups carrying blankets and cushions for the night's rest, with maybe a packet of food for an early breakfast.

One problem which seriously troubled the authorities was their knowledge that a direct hit on the pumps which carried water through subterranean London would flood the deep shelters and subways. Access to these shelters was forbidden until the people themselves forced entry and demanded protection regardless of this risk. And yet in spite of shelter facilities many people in the bombed areas continued to spend their nights in their own beds.

Most of the children in the great cities were evacuated to safer homes in the country. The wife, perhaps with her youngest child, sometimes stayed and took care of the husband but quite often the family left and the man lived alone in his home or in some hostel. Whatever the exertion of the day's work might be, every able-bodied civilian took his or her turn, often several nights a week, either in the home district or at the place of work, for duty as an air-raid warden, firewatcher to deal with incendiary bombs, first-aid nurse or ambulance driver. The life of the city had to continue; never once did its organisation become completely disrupted. People clung to the pattern of their lives as best they could, feeling that the life they led in the past helped them to keep their sanity in the madness of the present.

From June to December 1940 there were 166 days of continuous bombing on England. From September till December of that year there were 90 continuous days of raiding in the London area. It was not the single night of bombing that bothered people—it was the fatigue and the monotony, the sight of the injured and the dead, the pathetic exposure of the interiors of smashed homes, broken rooms with maybe a picture still hanging on the walls and torn curtains still up at the windows. The interrupted transportation and streets blocked with rubble made it difficult to get to work. For the women it was the everlasting queueing for whatever food was available, and the hard task of keeping house with windows smashed and broken roofs. There was no glass for replacement of windows, so tarpaulin, which kept out the light and let in the cold, was used instead. And always there was dust. The shabby and worn clothes; the drabness that comes from want of things; the shriek of sirens; guards in the factories to give the alert sign in the work hours; stumbling home in the black-out; shortage of light and fuel: all made a dreary picture for even the brave-hearted.

On the other hand as I look back on the days and nights of bombing I realise that in some curious way, despite fatigue, the effect of enemy action on most people was stimulating because it intensified the sense of urgency. And to those of us in the Embassy in this period, it made the war real for it gave us a feeling of sharing with the men and women who worked so untiringly in Britain's ordeal to survive. I shall never forget one night when I watched a fireman at the very top of an extension ladder fighting a fire on a high roof. The blazing building was a target for enemy planes, bombs fell around him but he carried on alone in his high post, a symbol of courage outlined in sharp silhouette against a sheet of flame. Although our country was not at war, and I was only a spectator, I felt, somehow, that we were with him and determined also to prevent this mad attempt to destroy what had been built up for the use of man.

Perhaps I can convey my own feelings by quoting a few lines from what I said at the English-speaking Union shortly afterwards. Senator George was kind enough to have them inserted in the Congressional Record at the time, and President Roosevelt used them later in a message accepting an honorary degree from Oxford University:

"Only this week in London, in the early morning hours of the Sabbath Day, enemy bombs destroyed the House of Commons room of the Parliament and smashed the altar of Westminster Abbey. These two hits seemed to me to symbolise the objectives of the dictator and the pagan. Across the street from the wreckage of these two historic buildings of State and Church, St. Gaudens' statue of Abraham Lincoln was still standing. As I looked at the bowed figure of the Great Emancipator and thought of his life, I could not but remember that he loved God, that he had defined and represented democratic government, and that he hated slavery. And as an American I was proud that he was there in all that wreckage as a friend and sentinel of gallant days that have gone by, and a reminder that in this great battle for freedom he waited quietly for support for those things for which he lived and died."

In an endeavour to prevent leakage to the enemy in reporting damage, many of the human incidents escaped notice at the time, though they came to be known later through the brilliant reporting of men like Wallace Carroll, who told the story of the fire in the "City." I, like all those who were in London during the raids, am acutely aware of the personal side, the small incidents that even now remain in memory.

One evening in the spring of 1941, just after my wife had arrived in London, we went to dinner with the Prime Minister and Mrs. Churchill. They were then living in the "Annex" in Whitehall. Although No. 10, Downing Street, had been trussed up to withstand bombing and was used in the daytime, at night the Prime Minister and Mrs. Churchill moved to the Annex, which was the nerve centre of the war control system. It was the first time I had been there, and after dinner Mr. Churchill took me down into the basement where I saw the communications and map room. The building, which housed these headquarters offices below ground, and the Prime Minister and his family on the first floor, was an administration building in Whitehall which had been reinforced with steel and concrete. It was a stronghold which could be held in the event of invasion and from which the direction of the High Command could be maintained.

I remember dinner as a pleasant family occasion, although we were all aware that there was a raid on. The Germans came over early that night. When it was time to leave, Mr. Churchill stepped outside with us. There was a complete black-out but for the searchlights sweeping the sky. Bombs were still dropping; we could hear the booming of the anti-aircraft guns and the rattle of shrapnel falling in the streets. Even in the dim light we could see the shimmer of rain on the pavements. Mr. Churchill arranged for our return in two armored cars. We went the rounds, leaving others of the party at their homes, and then returned to the Embassy. No damage had been done there.

I think it was a fortnight later that we had the heavy raid in which the bombs fell for the most part in Mayfair, the residential district surrounding the Embassy. We had two small shelters in the cellar of the Embassy which were used at night by the men and women who manned the code-room and others who were on night duty. I was working in my office that evening when the raid began. A small explosive bomb landed across the street and broke many of the windows of the Embassy. I remember the odd feeling of the drafts of cold night air in the room. My wife was upstairs in our flat. I went up there to suggest that she might like to go down to a shelter. But she was completely unafraid. She wanted to understand what people were going through, so she suggested we go up on the roof together to find out what damage was being done. From there we could see that two of the houses on the Square had been destroyed and that many of them were on fire from incendiaries. Over towards Oxford Street there was a blaze where the roof of a large department store had caught fire. Diagonally across from us a bomb fell which cut a house completely in half. Henry Stebbins, one of our officers who was living there, just happened to step out of his room before the bomb fell and this simple act saved his life. He was, however, trapped on the second floor because the stairs had gone. When he managed to get down by a ladder he came across to the

Embassy. By that time I had come down from the roof and he and I spent some time in my office trying to dust him off. When he took off his coat we found that it was heavy with plaster dust which had gone right through to his skin. It gave us something to laugh at, which always helps.

That same night an incendiary fell on the vacant Italian Embassy next door and some of our Embassy staff put the fire out. The next day I got a letter from the Brazilian Ambassador because at that time Brazil was acting for Italy as the "protecting power." This letter thanked us most politely for our services. I sent it on to Mr. Hull, feeling that it would amuse him to learn that our duties in London had included aid to the Italians.

Afterwards I went out and walked through the streets. I was struck by the number of houses ablaze which had to burn themselves out because of the lack of fire-fighting equipment. About this time the nine hundred fire districts of Great Britain were cut down to forty. These were so organised that they became mobile. This was done under the direction of Mr. Morrison, the Home Secretary. Immediately the direction of the night raiders was picked up by radar, the fire units massed in the area where the bombs could be expected to fall. But on this April evening in 1941 everybody was doing what he could to help the efforts of firemen and civil defense workers. I passed a building where the bodies of some trained nurses were being carried out. They had been trapped and killed. Only two blocks away I walked into an empty street full of brilliant firelight and the deep shadows of the black-out. There I came suddenly on a middle-aged woman standing at the door of her home. I spoke to her and in our brief exchange she said, "You know, my boy in the Navy came up for a week's leave from Plymouth and thought this was a dull place." And then she added with considerable pride—" But I certainly gave him an exciting time this evening."

It was not long after this raid that I wrote to the President:

"When you appointed me Ambassador you told me there were certain social phenomena which you wanted to know and which were seldom reported to you. Except for two week-ends with the Prime Minister and one with Beaverbrook I have not been able to get out of London. Therefore some of the things I am reporting I have not got at first hand. There are two things which have impressed me most: The first, the effort made to maintain the appearance of normal life in the face of danger, and the second, the patient acceptance of hardships and hazards by ordinary people. . . .

"You wanted to know the effect of bombing. At Clydeside a week or so ago eleven hundred persons were killed, sixteen hundred seriously injured and a very large number of homes destroyed. I was told by competent witnesses that while the families waited to be taken to what shelters were available, they rested on what little they had been able to save of their belongings, silent and grim 'without a tear in the lot.' An apprentices' strike which was going on was called off . . . individual output increased in the region. . . .

"The Germans are beginning to use heavier bombs. I saw photographs of the destruction in a workers' dwelling area caused by a 4,000-lb. German bomb. Four hundred people were killed and as many houses destroyed. . . .

"The air-raid shelters, while much improved, are still far from satisfactory."

It was in April that the Prime Minister asked Averell Harriman and me to go with him on a tour of some of the bombed areas. We went first by train from London to Swansea. In Swansea Mr. Churchill invited me to join him in his review of inspection. This included the Home Guard and other units. I also talked to dock workers and was struck by their courage and ability to improvise in spite of the destruction of equipment and dock facilities. We were in Swansea for a few hours only and then went by car to visit a secret weapons laboratory. On this occasion and at all times both before and after our entry into the war we were allowed to share freely in all military information and to see everything that was being done. At this laboratory I saw for the first time a proximity fuse bomb. It was later perfected by a group of American scientists working at Johns Hopkins University. It enormously increased the hits on the V1's—the winged German radio-controlled rocket projectile bomb—which otherwise would have done untold damage to London and in other areas in Great Britain and on the Continent. It proved an effective offensive weapon both in the Pacific and in the European theatre.

From Swansea we went on to Bristol by train, arriving in the early hours of the morning just at the end of a heavy raid. Fires were still raging and delayed-action bombs went off at intervals. In spite of this we found the people ready to receive us and they were able to go through the day's program as planned. We went directly from the train by automobile to the bombed districts. The fire brigades were busy, many streets were flooded from broken water mains or buried under rubble. Amongst all this the people were cooking breakfast in half-demolished houses or wherever a stove was functioning. I wrote the President that:

"I was deeply impressed by the response of the women, who might be described as the home makers, although many of them also do outside work. The Prime Minister's method of conducting a campaign on what one might call a morale front is unique. He arrives at a town unannounced, is taken to the most seriously bombed area, leaves his automobile and starts walking through the streets without guards. The news of his presence spreads rapidly by word of mouth and before he has gone far crowds flock about him and people call out to him, 'Hello, Winnie,' 'Good old Winnie,' 'You will never let us down,' 'That's a man.' I was interested to note that his 'Cheerio' in our earlier visits changed to 'God bless you' when we reached Bristol where people were still shaken by the bombing. The whole town was back on its feet again and cheering within two hours of his arrival, although no one had got any sleep during the night.

"On these trips the most marked determination and enthusiasm were among the middle-aged women who showed great appreciation of Mrs. Churchill's coming. If the future breeds historians of understanding, the service to Great Britain by the Queen and Mrs. Churchill will be given the full measure they deserve. Mrs. Churchill is a wonderful person and the look which flashed between her and these mothers of England was something far deeper and more significant than the casual newspaper accounts of social interchange. I often thought of Mrs. Roosevelt. It is very difficult for a man to interpret these emotions. However interested a man may be I had a feeling that in this task he was about as useful as a husband at childbirth."

I also remember that when we arrived in Bristol I was met by the American Vice-Consul, Waldo Bailey. He was swathed in bandages and confessed that in trying to help someone put out an incendiary he had fallen through a skylight and been badly cut.

When we went to the hotel we were all received by the Lord Mayor and Lady Mayoress quite according to plan, though only a few hours before they had been rescued by a boat from their home which had been flooded.

From the hotel we went on to Bristol University where many of the buildings were still smouldering. Here Mr. Churchill, as Chancellor of the University, presented honorary degrees to Mr. Menzies, the Australian Prime Minister; to Dr. Conant, President of Harvard University, in absentia; and to myself. The company were in academic robes, as is customary, but under them they wore a most extraordinary assortment of clothes. Some were in Service uniform, others in Civil Defence uniform, many in fireman's dress, and nearly all still soaked from their labors. They had been hard at it all night but all turned up. The Prime Minister on this occasion wore the robes which had been his father's when he was Chancellor of the Exchequer. We had gathered in a small hall because the large one had been damaged. The age-old ceremony went on against a new background. Through the windows we saw the smoke and flame and hoses of the firemen still playing on the burning buildings next to the University. And now and again we heard the crump of a delayed-action bomb. It was an impressive moment which Mr. Churchill sensed. On conferring the degrees he said, "I see a spirit bred in freedom, nursed in a tradition which has come down to us through the centuries, and which will surely at this moment, this turning-point in the history of the world, enable us to bear our part in such a way that none of our race who comes after us will have any reason to cast reproach upon their sires."

When I was asked to make a reply I fortunately remembered Burke's answer to the Sheriffs of Bristol, insisting on his right to defend the American colonies, which I still believe to be the greatest defense of representative government ever written.

I have other sharp memories of that morning. I remember with gratitude the cups of coffee and sandwiches which were given to us when we arrived at the University. I always marvelled at the way in which hot tea and food of some sort appeared as if by magic at the most difficult times during and after raids. There was a robed procession before the presentation of degrees and I remember that during it the wife of the Lord Mayor fainted. This seemed to underline the strain and nightmare of the recent hours.

When we were returning home on the train I was conscious of the sunlight and soft green of the English spring, startling in contrast to the bleakness of man-made destruction. Quite suddenly the Prime Minister turned to me and said, "I am going to see to it that the necessary tonnage is allotted for foodstuffs to protect them (the civil population) from the strain and stresses that they may be subjected to in this period of great emergency."

Only a few days before the Prime Minister and I had spoken at a combined meeting of Employers' and Workers' representatives. He had dwelt on the willingness with which trade unionists had accepted temporary suspension of privileges without which Britain would not have been able to produce under enemy fire the immense output of munitions necessary in order that soldiers, sailors, and airmen might battle on equal terms with the enemy. And I had suggested in reply that resistance required "not only skill, and hard work and materials in combination with the iron will of the soldier, but an understanding that is sensitive to the devoted loyalty of the people, and the determination to defend them in the efficiency of their giving." I was thinking of the acute rationing, of the great physical discomforts of life as much as of the actual labor.

In allotting more tonnage for foodstuffs I realised that Mr. Churchill had been deeply moved by what he had seen on this trip of the people's needs. At this desperate time there was always the temptation to cut down on food because of the compelling need for steel and armaments. When I wrote to the President of the Prime Minister's few words on the train I told him that I felt deeply that this policy of protection was necessary. I knew that he would fully understand.

V

THE EMBASSY

THE United States Embassy is at No. 1, Grosvenor Square. It is an old section of London. The architecture is predominantly Georgian. It is a place of early American tradition —the house occupied by John Adams on his mission to Great Britain still stands there and Walter Hines Page lived at No. 6 in the First World War. The square marked out a bit of America in this war and it is here that the British plan to erect a statue in memory of President Roosevelt.

In the Battle of Britain the lovely garden in the center of the square had been turned to more practical use. A group of W.A.A.F.'s and the blimp they called "Romeo" took shelter there. These W.A.A.F.'s were the first women's crew to man a blimp. They lived in low wooden huts which covered what were once flower beds around the parkway. Diagonally across from the Embassy, General Eisenhower later established his headquarters and Admiral Stark had a building next door which housed the naval mission. On the other side of the square were further military installations and offices occupied by the overflow from the Embassy itself. The Red Cross control under Harvey Gibson's able direction found a home in the square. The Japanese Embassy stood on one corner and the Italian Embassy was next to our own. Both were vacated when these countries decided to slink into war.

The United States Embassies in foreign lands are outposts

of American influence. Insofar as assignment of tasks to London permitted, everything was done to forward the democratic policies of the United States and, when war came, to support our military authorities.

In peace time the usual Embassy procedure had been to deal with the British Foreign Office only, with occasional contact with the British Treasury. There was also attached to the staff a representative of the United States Department of Agriculture, who reported on crop yields and whose assistants vetted livestock and examined plants that had been consigned for export to the United States. It was obvious that these limited procedures and relationships would be inadequate under the pressures of war. I therefore arranged with Anthony Eden, the Foreign Secretary, to deal directly with each Ministry concerned rather than follow the established ritual of channelling all contacts and negotiations through the Foreign Office. We accepted the obligation of informing the Foreign Office on any matter that involved any question of contract or treaty between the two countries. This was normally done in any event by the British agencies and our information served only as an added check which we were glad to supply. Always we kept our own government informed.

The emergency which obliged us to expand our contacts in this way also necessitated a wide knowledge and specialised skills which were not always available in the State Department. Consequently I asked Secretary Hull to allow other departments and agencies of the United States to appoint their own representatives to serve in the Embassy. It was agreed that I should be consulted concerning the individuals appointed, in order to maintain a working team, and that all communications to the departments and agencies in the United States should be cleared by me and passed through the Embassy code-room in order to avoid jurisdictional conflicts and prevent over-lapping. However, their authority and their current instructions stemmed from the departments and agencies which had assigned them to London. In this early period I was given complete authority to coordinate all civil and military activities. Everything was directed to keeping our military authorities informed. In carrying out its assignments, the Embassy did business with twenty-two ministries of the British government. After we had reorganised the Embassy to meet war conditions, we had a total staff of approximately 4,000. I can never be sufficiently grateful to the administration for the unusual ability of the special assistants assigned to the Embassy by the government departments.

The Embassy became an avenue of communications for the forwarding of British war experience, which was of immense value to the United States in the period of preparation before Pearl Harbor and afterwards. It also placed a special obligation on the Embassy to protect the information which was given us, and required a greater degree of security than would normally have been expected in those months before we engaged in war. It was about this time that a company of Marines was sent to London. They were assigned to guard the Embassy and the buildings occupied by the naval and military missions. They shared with the regular personnel the fire-watching and other civilian defense duties. Of the small company that were with us I have never seen men better trained, better behaved or more completely cooperative on a task that must have been irksome to them, during a period when our own country was not at war. Later when they were sent on to front-line duty we missed them very much. I was very proud when our younger son,

Riv, joined them in the Pacific. Churchill was quick to notice their coming and greatly enjoyed the words of the old Marine song:

> *"If the Army and the Navy ever look on Heaven's scenes,*
> *They will find the streets are guarded by*
> *The United States Marines."*

The waiting room at the Embassy was always crowded with people wanting to see somebody who had authority, quite apart from British Ministers, Ambassadors and other representatives of foreign governments who had official appointments. The saving grace for us was "Uncle Tommy"—Mr. Thomas Smith officially—who had been for more than a quarter of a century in the Embassy in London. His good nature, his courtesy and his sympathy were bywords at the Embassy.

In these first months we had a special duty to Americans who still remained in Great Britain and were anxious to return to the United States. Since our own ships were not permitted to enter combat zones and the repatriation ships were already taken off, we were dependent on British facilities for returning these Americans home. Space was scarce and there was always the decision as to whether you should risk American lives on ships in dangerous waters. We did not want another *Lusitania* tragedy. Most of those who were asking to return were women and children.

Another division in the Embassy dealt with the protection of British citizens and interests in enemy countries, which included transmitting information on prisoners of war and prison camps. The United States was then acting as the "protecting power" for Britain. When we got into the war, this responsibility was taken over by the Swiss, who acted for both the British and ourselves. The consideration of the Swiss for our prisoners of war in Europe, as well as the contribution made by the Swedish Government in the Asiatic theater, was a service that is sometimes forgotten, but will always be remembered by those of us whose sons fell into enemy hands.

Many of the refugees who escaped to Great Britain were trying to find their way to neutral countries, particularly the United States. This threw a heavy burden on our limited consular staff in the Embassy. In every United States Embassy and Legation I visited before we got into the war I found a shortage of personnel in the consular service which I was told was due to lack of appropriations. I found the same situation at the Embassy in London at the war's end.

Within a short time after my arrival in London we had missions attached to the Embassy which dealt with Lend Lease, economic warfare, scientific research, intelligence and subversive operations, information and psychological warfare and many other matters. In Washington at times there were jurisdictional differences among the parent organisations, but perhaps because we were in the war theater and working in the capital of another country, the men who worked in the various American missions in London managed to reconcile differences so we could present a united front in dealing with British authorities.

Shortly after I reached Great Britain and following the passage of the Lend Lease Act in March 1941, President Roosevelt appointed Averell Harriman as his "special representative" in London to expedite Lend Lease deliveries. He assigned him as Minister to the Embassy. It would have been hard to have made a happier choice. He established in the Embassy what came to be known as the Harriman Mission and, shortly after his arrival in London, Phil Reed came on as his assistant. Reed's experience in Washington with the War Production Board, as chairman of the board of one of the great international industrial enterprises, and as a lawyer and negotiator, were exceptional qualifications for this position. Together they, with an able staff, coordinated the needs of the British with the United States supply base. This entire concept originated with the President and with Harry Hopkins who was serving as Lend Lease Administrator. The assignment was carried out with skill, sagacity and tireless energy. Averell's wide experience in industry, in transport and in finance made him a unique choice for this position. Civil necessities and military needs were met with despatch, and the order of priorities showed a rare comprehension of the demands of total war.

President Conant of Harvard University and Ben Cohen, as I have already said, came over with me. The moral force of Conant's statements on the war issues was known and appreciated in Great Britain. I have always felt that his contact with the British scientists on this journey was the initial step in bringing about cooperation with the universities and laboratories of the United States. It was this pooling of scientific resources that was responsible for increasing and maintaining the overall lead in this vital field in modern war. Its contribution to victory cannot be over-estimated. President Conant, Dr. Karl Compton of the Massachusetts Institute of Technology, and Dr. Vannevar Bush, then Chairman of the National Defense Research Committee, I knew personally. All of them visited Great Britain. They, with other scientists, made contributions in the field of scientific warfare that carried through until the atomic bomb at Hiroshima ended the war with Japan.

The British had been quick to enlist scientists in the war effort. They were represented in the War Cabinet and sat with the British Chiefs of Staff. In the United States we had not, up to that time, given equal status to our men of science. I brought this matter to the President's attention several times.

Among the services we established in the Embassy was a unit which coordinated for American use scientific data given us by the British. We also made certain that all surgical advances in relation to wounds, burns and freezing were immediately transmitted to the United States. The information included research in tropical diseases. We found that the British had gone ahead of us in ballistics and in the development of explosive weapons. We reported on the use of radar in air and submarine control. We transmitted information on changes in British plane construction which enabled us to make alterations in our own airplane designs and on the faults of British tank treads which we eliminated from our own. There was no phase of fighting equipment, tactics or strategy that the British developed from their war experience that was not known to us before Japan struck at Pearl Harbor.

At the time of my appointment, I had asked that Ben Cohen be assigned to the Embassy as a special legal adviser. Before leaving Washington he had carefully documented the positions taken by the President, the Secretary of State, and the Congress, on the international situation. We had also made arrangements to get immediate information by cabled messages on any changes in policy or program. This was necessary because every day the political and military positions shifted to meet new emergencies which involved both factual and legal considerations in our relations with the British. It was necessary that I be informed and act promptly on new instructions.

When we first arrived the American mission attached to the Governments-in-Exile had not been established. Ben was a great help in his kindly treatment of those who had found asylum in London. His consideration for little people, as well as his informal contact with official representatives of the refugee governments, expressed America's real concern for the homeless and the defeated. When he left to take a special job for the President it was a great loss to me personally and to the work of the Embassy.

It was prior to my leaving Washington that the Allied Governments-in-Exile had set up their headquarters in London and that the London Embassy had established contacts with them. I had talked over with the President, at some length, the question of continuing this practise. It seemed to me then that the British contact alone was a full-time job, and that the heads of these governments, and their Secretaries of State and Ambassadors, would rightly feel neglected, if I were not easily accessible to them, or attempted to delegate someone in the Embassy to the important assignment of constant liaison with them, and through them with the resistance movements in each of their countries. There was also the possibility, while working closely with the British, of confusion and misunderstanding in reporting British attitudes to proposals put forward by the separate governments, while at the same time honoring our recognition of them by independently and impartially reporting back to Washington on proposals made by them to the United States government.

The President and Secretary Hull very wisely decided to establish an independent mission and appointed Anthony Drexel Biddle, who had previously served in Norway and Poland, as Ambassador in charge. It was established shortly after I reached London. No one could have been assigned to this difficult post who, in my opinion, would have carried it through to a more successful conclusion. I knew Tony Biddle at school and I was very fond of him. He was a great athlete and had a natural flair for leadership. I respected his industry and good sense, and his friendliness has been felt everywhere he has served. His home here was a haven for all those desperate people who for so many years were exiled from their homeland. The goodwill he and Margaret Biddle maintained in those days will never be forgotten by those who have the gift of kindly memory. When Biddle eventually gave up this post to take a commission in the United States Army, Rudolph Schoenfeld became Chargé d'Affaires, with the title of Minister.

It was later that Winfield Riefler came on as Minister in charge of Economic Warfare. He had had a wide experience while Professor of Economics at the Institute for Advanced Study at Princeton, as adviser to the United States Treasury and to the Department of Agriculture, and he also served on both the Financial and the Economic Committees of the League of Nations, with the approval of the Department of State. We had worked together both in Washington and Geneva. His experience and his integrity were responsible for establishing a relationship with the British that allowed us to work together in perfect partnership. The British had begun before we did to measure enemy indirect action in influencing neutral trade and shipping and before the war were engaged in the grim struggle to obtain strategic war materials that were in short supply. Such activities and many others, including sabotage, came within the scope and direction of these new divisions of economic warfare. The action taken by these agencies was often disturbing to the Foreign Office in Great

Britain and to our State Department in Washington, particularly in regard to our relationship with neutral countries. The Economic Warfare Division ran into conflicting jurisdictions with the Treasury at home, and at times was under fire from the War Department in regard to treatment of non-belligerent countries, but it did a useful and effective service. The economic warfare organisations countered the enemy in an area of activity that would not otherwise have been covered. They were essentially war instruments and both in Great Britain and the United States the agencies were abolished when the war ended.

I remember a typical incident of opposition to action taken in which I myself was involved. The selection of the targets to destroy German industry by bombing was largely determined by the reports of a research section of the British Ministry of Economic Warfare. When I found that these reports were used not only by the Royal Air Force but also by our own Air Command, I asked that American experts on German industry be attached to our London Economic Warfare Division in order that they might sit in with the British group in determining priority targets. Although I had the support of both General Spaatz and General Eaker in making this request through the State Department, Major-General Strong who headed G2 in Washington got the idea that I wanted to select American air targets from the Embassy! After some delay the issue was referred to General Eisenhower who took it up with me personally, and my suggestion was supported and approved.

In our great effort to be useful to the British many voluntary groups sent over observers to give assistance in one field or another. We tried to welcome everybody, knowing that the more people who understood war conditions here and could keep people accurately informed at home the better. Of course, we occasionally ran into British security officers who were rather bewildered by some of these wanderers who wanted to inspect everything from airfields to shelters, but I never heard of any harm coming from these excursions. Great good was accomplished by the contribution and the increased understanding of the visiting commissions and members of Congress.

The administration and the staff work of the Embassy were under a Minister assigned by the Department. The men who held this post were permanent officials belonging to the Foreign Service. Herschel Johnson was here when I arrived and stayed with me through the fall of 1941, when he became Minister to Sweden. He carried a heavy load and performed his duties with loyalty and distinction. I was new in the field of national diplomacy, and his consideration and unfailing help had much to do with the efficient working of the Embassy. He was objective in his estimate of people and during his seven years of service in London had come to know personally most of the men in the British Government. This proved of great help to me in my early contacts with the British Ministries. Later I had reason to be grateful to Freeman Matthews who succeeded him.

One occasionally hears criticism of foreign service personnel. I can only state my own experience. I am aware that our work fell within the theater of military operations and that in war we had the lifting force of a great unified command, but for all that I shall always be deeply conscious of and sincerely grateful for the competence, the courage and the loyalty of those I was privileged to serve with in London, whether civilians or soldiers.

VI

EDEN AND THE FOREIGN OFFICE

WHEN I reached London in 1941, Anthony Eden, Secretary of State for Foreign Affairs, was in the Middle East. I reported to Washington that I had missed his help. We had much in common. We had served as soldiers in the last war in the Allied Armies. Many of our friends fell in France. We had each in our own country supported the League of Nations from its inception. We had worked in the pre-war days in the international field to maintain the rule of law and social justice among nations. When we met in May, Great Britain was fighting for her life, the Western Front was smashed, and, in the free France of Lafayette and Foch, the tricolor had been torn down and the swastika flew over a conquered Europe.

Eden had been one of the few to understand and resist Mussolini. I remembered years before my own resentment at Mussolini's march on Rome, when he abolished the last semblance of representative government and set up a Fascist State. He destroyed the dreams of Mazzini, who had asked for "government of the people, for the people, by the wisest and the best." He threw away the sacrifices of Garibaldi and his thousand devoted followers. He turned the statesmanship of Cavour into a mis-shapen thing, and ruled Italy under blackshirted gangsterism. I could not bear the amused laughter of those in our own country at the sly cruelty of his castor-oil

61

treatment which ripped the guts out of the patriots of Italy. Nor could I hear without anger the extravagant praise of this man who was credited with knowing how to handle labor, and who delighted tourists visiting Italy, because trains ran on time and satin slippers were no longer soiled in city streets. All the while they ignored the fact that free men lay in prisons but a stone's throw from their comfortable hotels. Equally insidious was the blight that descended on the nation with the denial of free thought and freedom of expression which has left them unprepared to meet the responsibilities of democratic self-government. I had no use for this Dictator from Predappio, but I also feel that the manner of his death was an offence to those who respect liberty under law.

When Hitler used the same reactionary elements in Germany under cover of establishing national socialism to force his fuehrer rule, I had the same conviction that Nazism, as Fascism, would eventually wreck the peace of the world. Dictators as wantonly cruel to their own people as Hitler or Mussolini would inevitably be bereft of feeling for other peoples. It was equally clear to me that the evolution toward a friendly world called for a more positive policy of the democratic powers on a united front. Success in maintaining the peace requires unusual tolerance and surrender of selfish national aims. It means that we agree to do for others as we would be done by. These two men, in coming to power, turned back to the savage practices of the Dark Ages.

I remember William Dean Howells's son telling me that in the days when he was in college he had become discouraged by the selfishness and the hardness he found in the world of that day; but that his father reminded him that in spite of setbacks and slow progress, one of the certain evidences of advancement was the abolition of torture in the Western World during the preceding century. Everybody has bloodied his copybook in waging total war, but only Axis powers used scientific knowledge and mass-production methods in perpetrating "cruel and unusual punishments" on individual defenseless human beings. The terrible revelations of Belsen and Buchenwald place on record depravity, in a supposedly enlightened age, of a type and on a scale never before equalled. After the surrender the damning evidence of those camps could not be concealed or destroyed. Amidst the filthy ramshackle temporary huts crowded with human misery, rose the only permanently constructed buildings—the crematoriums with their large ovens. Humanity was once redeemed by the saying, "They know not what they do." These men not only knew, they planned, with cold premeditation, the slaughter of a race, and all others who opposed their will. Long before war came at all the indifference of an appeasement-minded world allowed these enemies of humanity, bereft of charity, an open field to sow and reap their nightmare harvests.

Similarly, the weakness of an appeasement-minded government had allowed Hitler and Mussolini to drive Eden from public office. He, Cranborne and Churchill, and a few others who represented the minority opinion, were swept aside as warmongers; warmongers because they had not forgotten the causes for which men had fought and died in the 1914 war. There was no doubt even in those early days that a free Europe was threatened by Nazi invasion. And yet in Great Britain and in Europe generally the people were still doubting and undecided. They hoped so desperately for peace.

The presence in the British Coalition Government after May 10th, 1940, of the men who had first sensed danger and who had determined to meet it was a guarantee of defense to the end. These men gave me their confidence because they knew I believed in their cause and in their will and ability to defend that cause, even while they stood alone.

The day Eden returned from Athens I saw him. He had been on a special mission with General Sir John Dill, Chief of the Imperial General Staff. The gallant Greek army had not only defended its own heroic people but had driven the Fascist Italian army back into Albania. They were, at that time, threatened by attack from mechanised German units which had occupied Bulgaria, and were menacing Yugoslavia. In spite of the precarious position in the Middle East, Eden, Dill and Wavell, with the support of the British Cabinet, agreed to withdraw land and air forces and send them to help Greece to reinforce its army against German attack. These troops were, for the most part, desert-seasoned veterans. After reaching this decision, Dill boarded his plane for England. As he stepped aboard, Wavell (who was Commander-in-Chief, Middle East Forces) turned to him and said, half laughingly and half sadly, "Jack, I hope when this action is reviewed you will be selected to sit on my court martial." All three men knew that at best it was a losing fight, but that if one had allies who stood up to the common enemy there was a moral obligation to support them, whether in victory or defeat. General Smuts, who had flown from South Africa at Eden's urgent request, shared their counsels and endorsed their judgment. Not one of them realised then that the resistance they planned in Greece, and the revolution in Yugoslavia which their action had encouraged, would sufficiently slow down the German advance to delay the attack on Russia until the end of June. For this the German armies paid a bitter price in the Russian winter of 1941–2.

The reputation of a statesman outside of his own country is often limited, nor does it always reflect a true picture of a man's worth. Many people at home liked Eden because he was good-looking, well dressed, conservative and a Britisher who frankly liked the United States. I found him a hard-working, unafraid Englishman who had spent his life in the service of his country. He was one of the best trained diplomats I have ever met. He had no use for shoddy politics whether at home or abroad. His views and his judgment on public affairs were based on knowledge and on a high sense of duty.

He came from an old county family from the North of England, and is a direct descendant of the Lord Baltimore who was responsible for the adoption of the Maryland Toleration Act. In the last war he left school, joined the 60th Rifles and was serving in France while still 18. His eldest brother, already a soldier, was killed in 1914. He himself came out of the war a major. His younger brother was a midshipman in the Royal Navy and was killed at the Battle of Jutland at the age of 16. After the armistice Eden went to Christ Church, Oxford, where he studied Oriental languages. He is a natural linguist and speaks fluently the languages of Western Europe. When he left the university he went into the Foreign Office. His first experience in diplomacy was in Persia, now Iran. He spoke the language, came to understand Persian politics and economy, and enjoyed their culture.

I had a great respect for his industry and his detailed knowledge of the voluminous despatches on foreign relations and military affairs that passed his desk. No one I know carried a heavier work load in the war. After serving as Secretary of

State for War in 1940, when he organised the Home Guard, he was made Foreign Minister in the Coalition Government under Mr. Churchill. He was also Leader of the House of Commons and the unnamed Deputy Defence Minister. Any of these three positions was a full-time job. He carried all of them, and used his command of foreign relations and his leadership in the Commons, with his knowledge of the military situation, to broaden policy, to strengthen understanding, to effect co-ordination, and to bring about unity of action.

The personal relationship between the Prime Minister and Anthony Eden was as close and real as President Roosevelt's friendship for Harry Hopkins. Roosevelt and Churchill, each a great leader single-minded in serving his country, understood that most men who crossed their doorsteps wanted something. Eden and Hopkins wanted nothing beyond being useful and loyal to a cause and a leader. They both had the courage to tell the truth, whether it was wanted or unwanted, to the men under whom they served. If this had been all they did the people of both countries would still owe them a deep debt of gratitude.

Eden was always on call, both day and night. He worked in the Foreign Office building. It was a great stone structure, ornate, with high ceilings, long corridors and with a formal staircase. Broken windows, which had been filled in with cloth, as well as imperfect lighting, gave a sense of darkness and dreariness to the place. It had few of the advantages of a modern structure and yet, like some old-fashioned concerns, it had stood the test of time. It was an efficient workshop because it was staffed with competent people, and there was about it a kind of old-world courtesy. The Foreign Secretary's personal office was on the north-eastern corner of the building, looking out on St. James's Park and across on to the new Admiralty building. It was a spacious room, cold in winter but light and cheery, well furnished and easily adapted for conference use. There was a side entrance to the building with an elevator which took you directly to his door. I used it to save time.

Like all other British Ministers, Eden lived on the job. He and his wife occupied a small apartment which had been an office on the top floor of the Foreign Office building. Twice it was blasted by bomb explosion, and the windows blown in. Luckily there was no one in at either time.

We had an odd informal relationship, based not only on personal friendship but also on our regard for each other's country and for our own. We both got satisfaction from working together for measures and actions that were of mutual advantage to both countries. In doing the day's work we tried to drop out the non-essentials of the usual diplomatic interchange and yet we were both exact in preparing formal agreements.

We used to go down occasionally on a Sunday to his country house in Sussex. It was not different from London as far as the work load was concerned, and we had the same long hours hooked up to a "scrambler" telephone, but instead of a room and a desk we used to go out into the garden. I have never known anyone who cared more about flowers or vegetables or fruit trees, or wind blowing across wheatfields, or the green pastures which marked out the Sussex Downs. We used to get our fun weeding the garden. We would put our despatch boxes at either end, and when we had completed a row we would do penance by reading messages and writing the necessary replies. Then we would start again our menial task, each in some subconscious fashion trying to find a sense of lasting values in the good earth.

I liked Eden. I found him simple, truthful and courageous. In those years before the United States became engaged in the war, he had two obsessions which I shared. He was determined, whatever the cost, not to involve his country in secret treaties, and never to repeat the British mistake in the last war when they made concessions to the Arabs which ran counter to their agreements under the Balfour Declaration. He never did. His entire foreign policy was based upon a high conception of moral right.

It had been customary for a Secretary of State for Foreign Affairs, after an interview with a foreign Ambassador, to take notes of the conversation and put them on record in the Foreign Office. Eden and I followed a different practice, for, as he said publicly after he left office:

"Quite early in our work together, Mr. Winant and I understood that we just could not get through our business if each interview between us—and sometimes there were two or more in a day—was to be the subject of a detailed record; and so we decided that normally there would be no record, unless we agreed that for the information of our respective governments, it was necessary to make one and repeat it to them. Such a practice and such a measure of confidence are unique in my diplomatic experience."

Perhaps this is an added reason for putting on record now the incidents and actions that may be useful to those who are to follow after us.

VII

DIFFERENCES BETWEEN THE
TWO GOVERNMENTS

ONE of the tasks of an Ambassador is to interpret correctly statements and decisions made by his government to those officially responsible in the country to which he is assigned, and to do a like service in transmitting messages from that government to his own government. I found on many occasions that the differences in our two forms of government were often responsible for confusion and misunderstanding. This was also true of public reaction in both countries.

The British and the United States Governments have similar objectives but they are conducted on different working plans. Although we have a common language, even words do not always have a common meaning, and the functioning of the day-to-day mechanics of administration does not run on the same time-table or, as the British say, s(c)hedule.

It is often difficult for the average Britisher to understand what we mean by a Federal system. They forget that we were originally thirteen separate colonies which each declared its separate independence and established in the New World thirteen sovereign states. It was the pressure of attack from outside, after we declared our independence, that prompted us to organise under the Articles of Federation. These Articles failed to delegate sufficient power to establish a new nation. When peace came and the pressure from outside ceased, the disintegration began, which was not unlike the breaking up of Allied unity after the First World War.

The test of statesmanship in those formative days was the realisation of this fact and a determination to establish a united nation. The men who had made possible our independence met and declared their purpose "to form a more perfect union" under a central government, which provided for "the common defense," and "the general welfare."

With us there is a tacit assumption that sovereignty is lodged in the people. We delegate authority under written contracts which we refer to as Constitutions, both in the several States and for the United States. The separation of powers of the Executive, the Legislative and the Judiciary was common to both the States and the Federal Government and designed to safeguard the liberties of the people. This division of authority was referred to as a system of "checks and balances." The right of judicial review was later exercised by the courts. They can declare a statute passed by a Legislature or the Congress after approval by the Executive, as lying beyond the powers granted under a written Constitution and, therefore, null and void.

This is quite a different plan of government from the British, which is based on an unwritten constitution with sovereignty or supreme power in the Parliament. The Acts of Parliament stand as the law of the land and are not subject to judicial review. The King is the head of the State. In him the affections and the loyalties of the people are centered, while the practical working functions of government are exercised by the Cabinet and the Parliament. Thomas Jefferson was able to force recognition of a "constitutional opposition," but we use no phrases equivalent to "His Majesty's Government" and

"His Majesty's Opposition." In Great Britain loyalty is owed to the Crown; with us it is an idea symbolised by the flag—as Justice Holmes put it, "Its red is our life blood, its stars our world, its blue our heaven."

These differences have their outward and visible distinctions. The British show a greater deference to the King than we do to the President. We stand at attention or, as civilians, lift our hats when the flag passes; it is taken down when it is raining, and when we "strike the colors" at sundown we do not let it touch the ground. We both stand when our national anthems are played. I do not want to labor this comparison, but common courtesy requires mutual understanding. I remember an American colonel coming into the Embassy indignant because he had seen an American flag hanging in the rain upside down from a neighboring window. I took the trouble to find out the reason. Two elderly people had bought an American flag out of hard-earned savings in order to show their appreciation to American soldiers who had just arrived in Great Britain. Even the best of goodwill sometimes leads to misunderstanding if we are not aware of the practices and customs of other countries.

I had not been in London long before I sensed a certain resentment on the part of newly arrived American press representatives because Mr. Churchill refused to hold weekly press conferences. From their point of view it certainly seemed a reasonable practice, since the President met the press twice weekly. It was through the press and the radio that he kept the American people informed. They had elected him Chief Executive and he was directly responsible to them. The Prime Minister, on the other hand, is the leader and the servant of Parliament. Members of the House of Commons would have deeply resented Mr. Churchill by-passing them and directly reporting through the press to the people. In the most trying days of the war, when all the Prime Minister's energies were spent in its prosecution, some members suggested that a radio installation might be brought into the House of Commons in order that his address on the state of the war might be heard by the public. The idea was rejected by an almost unanimous vote of the House. Tired and worn as he was, he had to repeat his message to an anxiously waiting people in an evening broadcast.

British executive authority stems out of its legislative branch of government. The Cabinet, which is selected from the Houses of Parliament and formed under a Prime Minister on a directive from the King, must have the confidence of the House of Commons and be supported by a majority of its members. Cabinet members retain their seats in Parliament. Where decisions called for action by both the executive and the legislative branches of government, they were more rapidly resolved under the British system of government than was possible with our division of executive and legislative powers.

In the war years, under a Coalition Government, major policy was entrusted to a selected group of the Cabinet, known as the War Cabinet. The unity of authority between the legislative and the executive branches of government also permitted a greater coordination of action. Overall control was further strengthened by the Chiefs of Staff sitting in with the War Cabinet on matters that affected the actual conduct of the war. A single Secretariat served both the Cabinet and the Chiefs of Staff. The Prime Minister took over the office of Defence Minister.

The First Lord of the Admiralty, the Secretary of State for

War, and the Secretary of State for Air, reported directly to the Defence Minister and were not themselves members of the War Cabinet, although they were normally present for the items on the Cabinet agenda that had to do with the conduct of the war. The Cabinet had over twenty members, a third of whom served in the War Cabinet. The Secretariat was composed of some fifty members made up of able young civilians and officers. They were interchangeable on both civil and military assignments.

The British have developed what is known as "responsible Cabinet government." No major decisions of policy were taken in the war that had not the approval of the Cabinet, although the details of military operations were revealed only to the Defence Committee, over which the Prime Minister presided, and to which a few selected ministers and the Chiefs of Staff belonged.

Churchill's genius was in his capacity as a democratic leader. He was always a good House of Commons man. He never took a decision that bound his country without Cabinet consent. His dominating influence, whether in the Cabinet, or the Commons or the country, came from his ability to state his case and marshal majority support.

There has been a shallow acceptance among some people in the United States, and a few in Great Britain, that he was a Tory determined only to defend the British Empire and was indifferent to the exploitation of dependent people.

My own belief in him was based on the conviction that he was, in fact, an old-fashioned Whig. He is himself a Free-Trader. I believe if he had lived in the time of George III he would have joined with Chatham, Fox and Burke in defense of the colonies against the King and Lord North. In our time he has fought to defend the rights of man. I knew no one in Great Britain as much troubled as he was by the necessity of imposing Defence Regulation 18B, which suspended Habeas Corpus and permitted arbitrary arrest without trial by jury. This action was justified under the emergency of a threatened invasion, but it meant the temporary suspension of long-won freedoms.

He fully realised the restraints necessary in exercising the sovereign powers of Parliament. He was always keenly aware that the established rules and procedures in the Commons were safeguards against the arbitrary use of power. His profound knowledge of their historic background allowed him to see clearly that they represented man's slow progress toward self-government under law. He never breached them. They represented restraining influences which he expounded, subscribed to and defended. I have heard him say again and again that "power corrupts." Always he was on his guard against the abuse of power. He went further because he knew in his heart that justice should be tempered with mercy.

It was, however, the duty of the Prime Minister to use the power which Parliament and the nation had given him to drive others and, in a war of self-preservation, as he said, "that power has to be used irrespective of anyone's feelings. If we win, nobody will care. If we lose, there will be nobody to care."

In the British House of Commons, a question of confidence can be raised by the Government or by the Opposition and an adverse vote would mean the defeat of the Government and the resignation of the entire Cabinet. This ensures joint responsibility and team play while a Government is in office. All stand together or fall together.

There were times when the Prime Minister was criticised for forcing "votes of confidence," and yet I believe he will be completely justified in retrospect. There was absolute freedom of debate. The attacks of the minority membership were often violent and plausible. On the occasions when a measure supported by the Cabinet had been subjected to critical attack the Coalition Government would, in my opinion, have been weakened if the issue had not been drawn and a vote taken. Churchill was never willing to accept the view that the particular issue was immaterial to the prosecution of the war. The smashing majorities he received whenever he forced a vote or asked for reconsideration, on a vote of confidence, in my judgment, lifted the Allied cause and discouraged the enemy.

The Parliament Act of 1911 limited tenure of office to five years, but this was superseded by the Prolongation of Parliament Acts during the war emergency. These measures permitted the members of the House of Commons to continue in office for nine years without an election. The same practice was followed in the First World War. This flexibility is in marked contrast to our more limited terms of office in the United States, and the constitutional requirements of holding elections at fixed periods of time. The uncertainties which were inevitable in the national election in the United States in 1944, and the conflict of opinions which divided the people in the campaign, were disturbing to the Coalition Government in Great Britain and a confusion to the British people. We took them in our stride and strengthened our unity of purpose, in my opinion, by holding a fresh mandate from the people in the closing year of the war.

Under the British procedure a speech made by a Cabinet

Minister is dictated by the policies agreed upon by the entire Cabinet and is not the expression of the personal opinion of the Minister himself, but a public announcement of government policy. In the summer of 1941 when Secretary Stimson made a belligerent speech attacking the Axis powers, there was a general assumption in Great Britain that the United States was moving toward an immediate declaration of war. I remember the following day we were kept busy at the Embassy answering telephone calls and other enquiries to clarify the situation. The Secretary had simply expressed his own opinion of the policy he believed the United States should pursue, although he had spoken undoubtedly with the President's full consent and approval. A statement by a Cabinet member in our government could not be interpreted as a declaration of war. Only the United States Congress has power to declare war.

There are other odd bits of detail that are not always understood. In the absence of Ministers the Parliamentary Under-Secretaries, who are political rather than Civil Service appointees, take over the duties of office. This is similar to the practice followed in the United States. When the Foreign Minister, however, leaves the country, the responsibility for foreign affairs goes to the Prime Minister. He may take over the office himself or delegate it to some other Minister. And again, in the Foreign Office the next ranking official to the Minister is the Permanent Under-Secretary, who is the top civil servant. During the war, because of the heavy pressure in the Foreign Office, an additional secretary with the rank of Minister of State was appointed to the Foreign Office by the Prime Minister. His major duties had to do with work affecting international economic and social problems.

As John Morley said long ago, the Foreign Office lies within the province of the Prime Minister, although, under the unwritten Constitution of Great Britain, the Foreign Minister is in the highest sense a constitutional officer.

Under the written Constitution of the United States the President "shall have power by and with the advice and consent of the Senate to make treaties, provided two-thirds of the Senators present concur; and he shall nominate and, by and with the advice and consent of the Senate, shall appoint Ambassadors, other public ministers and consuls. . . ." The office of Secretary of State and the Department of State were created by the Congress. The Secretary of State is appointed by the President, subject to confirmation by the Senate.

The method of granting appropriations which normally would appear to be a purely domestic matter has, on occasion, upset our relations with the British. Monies in the United States are appropriated by the Congress, and because of the separation of executive and legislative functions where approval is given, the Congress makes specific appropriations for specified amounts. In Great Britain, because the executive and the legislature are merged, it is the practice of the Parliament to authorise general credits and the Chancellor of the Exchequer simply informs the House of Commons of the use to which these available monies will be put. No particular item requires special authorisation. I remember when we had reached agreement on U.N.R.R.A. contributions, the administration at home was very much disturbed because a specific allocation for relief funds had not been made by the Parliament. It just was not the British way of making an appropriation and yet there was complete good faith on both sides and each country made its quota contribution on time and up to the full amount agreed.

Another confusion that we were able to correct at short notice was due to the fact that the communications in relation to the decisions of the Cabinet were often transmitted through the Minister whose department was concerned, and addressed to his counterpart in the United States. The Minister in question might have done his utmost in the Cabinet to get a favorable decision to meet the request of our government, but without success. The fact that he sent in the negative report, however, would often bring down on him the wrath of our resentment, much to the amusement of the dissenting members of the Cabinet who were responsible for the negative action taken. In my opinion one of the most important elements in international relations is to know who the true friends of your country are in other governments and to do what can be done to make their trust and confidence a help to them in their effort to establish good relationships.

The clear authority delegated under the Constitution of the United States and by statute to the Executive, which included war powers, allowed wide discretion of action within the administrative field. This permitted quick decision when joint British-United States executive action was required and often gave us a time advantage in dealing with the British ministries, for in spite of the wide powers exercised by the Cabinet, the obligation of consultation was always inherent under their procedure. We would sometimes demand an immediate answer on an issue that had not the prior approval of the Cabinet and be impatient because of the delay in answering, not realising that the reply could not be made until the item had been put on the Cabinet agenda and, after explanation and discussion, had been approved, amended, or rejected. The usual practice was to allow such matters to wait over until regular Cabinet meetings because it was difficult in the war period to summon special meetings without dislocating the work of administration. This was done, however, on emergency matters of major importance.

Ever since the time of Cromwell, Parliament has jealously protected its rights and prerogatives, and civil authority has supremacy over the military services. It is outside usual British practice to delegate political authority to the military. This does not mean that British officers are not informed on the political policy of their government, or that they are not under obligation to carry forward such policy. In the North African campaign, in which we had insisted on unity of command under General Eisenhower, we assigned Robert Murphy as political adviser. He reported through General Eisenhower to the State Department. He held the diplomatic rank of Minister. The British, on the other hand, assigned Harold Macmillan, a Cabinet Minister, as political observer who reported back to the British Cabinet. In this instance the accommodation to meet our two different concepts of political and military control, which was complicated because we were operating in Unoccupied French territory, was personally worked out by Roosevelt and Churchill. The President, by precedent and law, is free to delegate both military and political authority to a General in command in any theater of war. The British hesitate to do this. The separate authority given to Oliver Lyttelton in his assignment as Minister of State in the Middle East while retaining his position as a member of the War Cabinet is another example of a different concept of command and political responsibility. We do not assign members of the Cabinet to overseas posts.

On one occasion I was asked to address the Constitutional

Club. About this time there had been a series of military disasters, and a section of the press, with some support from the House of Commons, was urging that Churchill give up his position as Defence Minister, and limit his activities to the usual prerogatives exercised by the Prime Minister. The dissenting group also argued that the control of the war should be put into the hands of a smaller War Cabinet of four or five men who would hold office without portfolio, and be relieved from the administrative responsibilities of a Ministry. This plan was put in operation after Lloyd George took over from Asquith in 1916. Churchill would have none of it. He did not want a lot of "idea men" around who were freed from the sobering responsibilities of administering a section of the war machine.

I knew of his great contribution as Defence Minister and of the respect the British Chiefs of Staff had for his knowledge of war. They clashed with him at times, and on occasion held different views, but this man knew the composition of every military unit, the calibre of every shell, the thickness of the skin of every battleship, every type of airplane, the use of every instrument of war, and had a clear overall concept of war. In talking with him they did not have to translate military ideas into lay language. He listened to and sought expert advice, and in the end, with few exceptions, accepted the judgment of his Chiefs of Staff. He had the greatest respect for our own military leaders.

Just as I was leaving my car to keep this engagement at the Constitutional Club, I found that many of those who were supporting the abolition of the functions of Defence Minister were to be present. I tore up my set speech and decided I would talk extemporaneously on the differences between our two governments. I spoke for more than an hour, with but a single purpose. It was to explain that in the United States the President was both the Chief of State and the Chief Executive, and that in Great Britain the King was the Head of the State, with the Prime Minister exercising certain executive functions; that under the Constitution of the United States, the President was the Commander-in-Chief of the armed forces, which was not true of the Prime Minister; and finally that the Prime Minister, in taking over the position of Defence Minister, was able to deal more nearly on a basis of equality with the President on war matters than if these responsibilities were scattered. The President's problem was simplified in dealing with a single responsible leader. It would have been impossible for him to have made day-to-day joint decisions directly with a Committee of the Cabinet. In the weeks following I did not see again in print nor hear of further reference to opposition to Mr. Churchill as Minister of Defence.

I had remembered in the last war General Pershing's insistence that our troops were not to be brigaded with either the French or the British armies and so lose their identity as an American army under an American commander. This was a sound decision at that time which had the support of the American people. But I had not forgotten Marshal Foch's statement when the war was over that he had lost much of his lifelong veneration for Napoleon. Napoleon, he said, only had to fight coalitions and, as far as Marshal Foch could see, any reasonably efficient general could defeat a coalition. He was not speaking of coalition government within a nation, where political partisanship was put aside and everyone served the national will, but of the loose military coalitions between allied governments with their national armies and their unwillingness to share fully in planning united attack against a common foe.

It seemed to me in this war that we wanted more than this type of military coalition if we were successfully to meet the integrated forces under the German High Command. This idea was in alignment with later United States military policy which centered complete responsibility on a single commander in each theater of war. I believed that the realization of such a program would in large measure be dependent upon the personal relationship between President Roosevelt and Winston Churchill, Prime Minister and Minister of Defence of Great Britain.

If we had been deprived in this war of the constant and confident relationship between Roosevelt and Churchill we would have been denied the tremendous contribution made by the Combined Chiefs of Staff and a unified command in Europe under General Eisenhower.

Nor was this all, for what was true of a common battle front I was certain would be equally true of a common peace front. It had always seemed to me that the formality and the rare interchanges between President Wilson and the two war Prime Ministers of Great Britain, Asquith and Lloyd George, left the British and ourselves far apart when we met to negotiate peace in Versailles in the summer of 1919. In spite of Wilson's heroic individual effort to create a world organisation, the accumulation of unresolved differences that had neither been canvassed nor discussed in daily interchange in the war years left American public opinion unprepared to accept the compromises necessary to consummate a peace and to ratify the League of Nations Charter. In saying this I realise the enormous difficulties in setting up for the first time an organisation "to promote international cooperation and to achieve international peace and security"* in the world.

It is understandable that in facing up to political and military issues during this war and attempting to thrash them out in the day's work that differences appeared; but because they were dealt with daily across the table and over the cables, we developed a common battle front and a mutual understanding on a common peace front.

I remember when Churchill returned from the Atlantic Charter meeting in August 1941 members of the Cabinet went to the London station to meet him with Ambassadors of the Allied countries. His family went into the railway car to greet him. When he stepped out of the car he saw me in the crowd and came across to shake hands, with the simple statement, "I like your President." He never changed—he liked him to the end. Whenever I talked with the President I felt the same sense of caring on his part.

During the war years I handled the messages that passed between Roosevelt and Churchill. No matter how sharp the differences of opinion were between them, there was always courtesy and consideration—each trying to help the other and yet realising their individual responsibilities were not always the same. Both had an unconquerable courage—the President kindly and determined, the Prime Minister forceful and magnanimous. I do not believe that in the annals of history the leaders of two great nations were ever more true to their own people or so completely devoted to a common cause.

The spirit and the willingness to sacrifice were there in the war years. Roosevelt is dead now and Churchill no longer in power. We still have the framework that they so painfully

* Preamble to the Covenant of the League of Nations.

pieced together; what we do with it depends upon the capacities of those now responsible for government in the world to-day.

It is impossible to leave a comparison between the two governments without reference to the overall differences between the United States and the British Commonwealth and Colonial Empire. The States of the United States and its possessions under our own federated system make up a single unit for dealing with all external affairs including the treaty power, defense, and the tax authority necessary to their support. The exercise of these powers is the responsibility of the centralised government in Washington.

The British Commonwealth presents a different picture. The control of the British Isles, with the exception of Eire, is centred in London. Since the Imperial Conference of 1926 and the acceptance of the Statute of Westminster in 1931, it has been recognised within the Commonwealth that it is composed of self-governing dominions of His Majesty the King, each in all respects of sovereignty equal to each other, and all of them separately responsible for policy in internal and external affairs. The tie that binds them together is of the spirit rather than legalistic or material. It is loyalty to the Crown and a common heritage.

The external affairs of the United States are the responsibility of the State Department. The territories and possessions of the United States are administered by the Interior Department. The external affairs of the United Kingdom and the Colonies are the concern of the Foreign Office, but it is as well for us to remember, to avoid confusion, that relationships with the Dominions are under a separate Ministry—the Dominions Office; the Minister for the Colonies has to do with Colonial affairs; there was also a separate Ministry for India; Northern Ireland, which has its separate executive and legislative branches of government, comes under the Home Office.

When war came the treaty-making power, defense and the cost of it, were the separate responsibilities of each of the Dominions, including Great Britain. Each separately declared war. The loyalty to the Crown, combined with self-interest, prompted each and all of them to consolidate on a common front of defense and offense. In the early years of the war the overall plan for defense was centered in London, and since Great Britain was first in the line of attack the other Dominions came at once to her aid in contributing both men and materials. It was also the stronghold of the Empire.

After war broke out, the procedures and machinery for communication and consultation between the Dominions were inadequate for the new burdens that were inevitably thrown upon them. In wartime, events move with lightning rapidity. Vital decisions have often to be taken at a few hours' notice. Moreover, in the Second World War, the coordination of defense and supply presented new problems of the most formidable kind. It was therefore found necessary to elaborate still further the means of communication and the machinery for consultation. On the political side, the flow of messages from London to the other Dominion capitals, and from these to London, enormously increased. In 1944, for example, no fewer than 24,966 telegrams were handled by the Dominions Office. Each day, the information which came from the foreign missions abroad was passed on to the Office of External Affairs in the Dominions capitals. In addition, there was daily consultation with the High Commissioners who represented the other Dominions in London and in other capitals, on matters which were better dealt with orally than by official cables between governments. Another channel of consultation was by direct communications between Prime Minister and Prime Minister, on questions of the most confidential nature. Finally, there were instituted in London daily meetings between the Secretary of State for Dominion Affairs and the Dominions High Commissioners, at which he read to them the most secret telegrams and explained the views of his Cabinet colleagues on all developments in the war situation, as and when they occurred. In this way, the High Commissioners were enabled to keep their governments constantly informed as to the background of events. In order to perform this function, the Dominions Secretary always attended meetings of the War Cabinet, even when he was not a member of that body. There were also periodic visits by Dominions Prime Ministers, other Ministers and high officials to London, and by United Kingdom Ministers and officials to Ottawa and other Empire capitals, when that was practicable. And so far as Australia was concerned, Mr. Stanley Bruce acted as representative of the Australian Government to the United Kingdom War Cabinet. It was by this elaborate network of consultation that the views of the Dominions governments were always obtained before any important decision was taken. There were one or two occasions when the necessity for immediate decisions made this impossible. But these occasions were very rare and, broadly speaking, the British Commonwealth coordinated both its information and its action.

Side by side with the direction of the political policy went the military conduct of the war and the administration of supply. The service and supply departments of the various governments had missions in the other capitals of the Commonwealth. These sat together on committees and, under instructions from their governments, administered the joint war effort. When necessary, the responsible Ministers came themselves to London to settle difficult points. So complicated an organisation could not have been operated without the cable, the airplane and the radio. It needed all the resources of modern invention to make it effective or indeed possible. But it worked, and on the whole it worked well.

All this, in spite of every effort to expedite business, occasionally slowed down military operations and delayed allied decisions. The Dominions governments were responsible to their people for the troops recruited within their countries. Therefore, every operation which utilised the armed forces of the Commonwealth had to have the general approval of the home countries of the troops involved. I also remember Marshal Stalin's difficulty in understanding that a treaty between the Soviet Union and Great Britain could not be approved without consultation with the other Dominions governments.

India presented a different problem. It was neither a Dominion nor a Colony, but being under British control, its defense was an Imperial responsibility. There was an automatic declaration of war. Indian opinion was not consulted.

At this time, India was divided into British India on the one hand and the Indian States on the other. The Viceroy combined two appointments—to the British Provinces he was Governor-General, to the Indian States he was the Crown Representative. In both capacities he was Viceroy-Representative in India of the King. The British Provinces were administered by Governors appointed by the King. Every Province had legislatures consisting of elected members and responsible ministries exercising similar powers and privileges to the legislatures in the Provinces within the Dominions. The Indian Princes had their own armies and their own administrative services. There was a Chamber of Princes of which the Viceroy was President.

Simultaneously with the declaration of war on Germany, there began the enlistment of the greatest voluntary army in history. By the end of 1941, the Indian Army had expanded from a total of 189,000 men in 1939 to one of nearly one million, with an expeditionary force of 200,000 men overseas. The strength of the Royal Indian Navy and the Indian Air Force multiplied six and eight times during this period. The supply services of India also made great contributions to the war effort.

In London, two representatives, one for British India and one for the Indian States, joined Dominions representatives in the British War Cabinet.

I was often struck by the patience and the conscientiousness of the home government in its constant striving to keep the members of the Commonwealth fully informed and to act in complete consort with them. It showed great regard in honoring the obligations of a democratic system of government; but these continuing consultations occasionally created an impression of procrastination in dealing with us when we were anxious to get a job done with the least possible delay.

The war relationship between Great Britain and the Colonial Empire was on a still different basis. Although many of the Colonies had been granted self-government in their respective areas, they were not responsible for foreign policy, and the coordination of Colonial defense was an Imperial, not a local, responsibility.

The Colonies entered the war in the same state of unpreparedness as Great Britain and the rest of the Commonwealth. As the war developed, and as more and more countries fell under the Axis domination, certain Colonial areas assumed great significance in the pattern of the Allied war effort, for strategic bases, convoy assembly points, sources of raw material and reservoirs of manpower. These assets were of material aid to combined Allied military operations. The normal peacetime machinery by which the greater part of official business was conducted between the Colonial Office in London and the Colonial governments had to be reorganised to meet the unprecedented and urgent needs of war. Many of the newly-created wartime departments of state became vitally interested in the task of mobilising the resources of the Colonies to step up the production and supply of war material of all kinds, and the general conduct of economic warfare.

Another important feature of the machinery set up to deal with the conduct of the war, and questions of supply, was the creation of regional organisations in certain Colonial areas. In West Africa a War Council dealt with matters relating to the conduct of the war. These activities were co-ordinated by Lord Swinton, a former Secretary of State for the Colonies, appointed in 1941 as Resident Minister in West Africa with Cabinet rank and direct access to the Prime Minister. In East Africa the Governors' Conference, which had existed in peacetime, was reorganised and strengthened to include Supply Councils and the necessary machinery for liaison with the military authorities. In the West Indies the Caribbean Commission similarly dealt with wartime supply matters.

These organisations, which may well prove to be the fore-runner of a gradual evolution of British Colonial policy in the direction of large administrative units, played a valuable part in ensuring full Colonial contribution to the war effort. The East and West African territories alone put into the field 350,000 men, who fought in East Africa, in Madagascar and later in Burma. On both sides of the African continent the production of many vital war materials was substantially increased. They included copper, manganese, bauxite, rubber, sisal, quinine and oil seeds. Their value to the Allied war effort as the war progressed was of the highest importance. The oil products of West Africa provided over 40 per cent of Great Britain's fat ration; the sisal products of East Africa provided more than half the United Nations' supply of hard fiber.

This machinery, which reached a high degree of efficiency, would, however, have had far less effective results if it had not rested on the firm foundation of the loyalty and goodwill of the Colonial peoples themselves toward the mother country, and the general Commonwealth and Colonial concept which includes in principle the evolutionary realisation of self-government and eventual Dominion status. From Jamaica to West Africa, from West Africa to Fiji, Colonials flocked to the standard in their thousands. And those whose circumstances did not allow them to fight stayed at home and worked.

It should also be noted that even with all the difficulties of war, the United Kingdom Government pressed forward its policy of Colonial development. In 1940, while the Germans were swarming around the Channel ports, Parliament passed the Colonial Development and Welfare Act providing £50 million for a ten-year program of social and economic development in the Colonies.

In the years I was in the International Labor Office I worked hard for the objectives which this measure set out to accomplish. Shortage of manpower hampered the full operation of the program, but much useful work was done, which included the preparation of many plans for the future.

In the Caribbean we shared these plans. Both before and after the Base-Lease Agreement, I urged a joint approach by both the British and ourselves to implement the recommendations of the West Indian Royal Commission Report and the Taussig Report on our West Indian possessions. These efforts led to the establishment of the Anglo-American Caribbean Commission. I felt that this area, which was in our front yard and related to our coastal defense, might be used not only to improve conditions for the inhabitants of the islands, but also to develop new methods to raise standards of living in other colonial and non-self-governing territories.

The final years of the war brought some benefit but also much hardship to these island people for whom we both held a primary responsibility. Their one crop economy, stripped of transport, left some in precarious circumstances. The demand for labor in the Base-Lease areas was temporary and too few communities supported a self-sustaining agricultural economy. Much good was accomplished by our joint action, but there is still far more to be done by the great democracies to work out a good life for those who earn their living on the fertile lands that are washed by the lovely waters of the Caribbean. I believe this area could be made an example to all the world of what Colonial government might be. At least it is a testing ground in which the Colonial Powers can prove their good faith to under-privileged people in the world of to-day.

I believe in the main the effect of the war was to strengthen the ties between Great Britain and the Colonies, and to increase goodwill and mutual understanding.

At a time when colonial empires everywhere are under constant fire of criticism, it is well that these relationships should be remembered and recorded.

VIII

LEND LEASE AND FOREIGN EXCHANGE

Now I want to speak about the making of modern war, and look at the relative position of Great Britain to Germany and Italy in manpower, armaments, food, trade and foreign purchasing power at the outbreak of the war.

In order to get a correct measure of the time it is necessary to go back to the pre-war period rather than be wise after the event. It helps, also, to tie together many apparently unrelated and isolated facts in trying to evaluate correctly the importance of Lend Lease. The Prime Minister described it as the "most unsordid act in the whole of recorded history." It is probably true that no act of a neutral power ever contributed more to the defeat of an aggressor nation. The Lend Lease program was before Congress when I left the United States. It had been recommended by the President in his Annual Message to Congress. It was approved by large majorities in both Houses and became law on March 11th, 1941.

Lend Lease was an invention of the President that opened the way for giving immediate and effective aid to those defending democracy, and it was designed to avoid the aftermath of debt obligations which led to so much distrust and economic dislocation after the First World War. It allowed us in that bleak December of 1941 to join with allies better equipped and more powerful because of our aid, and it was because of the earlier British war orders and Lend Lease that industry and agriculture within the United States were already moving on a war basis. Lend Lease was a practical measure. We could not say after declaring war that, "We've got the ships, We've got the guns," and the airplanes, the tanks and all else, but we did have the plants to build them on a scale never before realised, and we had the men and "the money too."

There was another consideration in developing the war industries in the United States that was important and understood. The German war industries were based on machine tools. They were the foundation for their industrial war machine. The industry in the United States that had done most in using machine tools to develop mechanised output was the automobile industry. The selection by the President of William S. Knudsen from the automotive industry was proof of that understanding. The contribution made by Knudsen to modernise industry through the intelligent use of machine tools and their directed allocations had much to do with the phenomenal production that amazed our allies and dismayed our enemies.

All this practical side of war reminded me of General Grant's messages to the War Department when he made his way down the Ohio River. He was forever writing about mules and wagons and shoes for his soldiers, while other generals who were doing less fighting were discussing tactics and Jomini * and all the jargon of theoretical warfare.

And then I thought of George Marshall. Grant would have comprehended the man—this tall figure who could grasp the total reach of war with practicality, imagination and global-mindedness.

* Baron Henri Jomini, French military authority, 1779–1869.

I loved the courtesy he showed to General Pershing, his old commander. You did not need to be told that he would have the courage to pick a Lieutenant-Colonel, Dwight D. Eisenhower, and put him in command of the European Theater of Operations, or that he would generously support General MacArthur, who had once been his superior, as the Commander-in-Chief of the Pacific.

I remember Churchill turning to me toward the end of the war and saying, "Perhaps he was the greatest Roman of them all." This man knew the art of modern war; and what we owe to him future generations will measure to his credit long after we are gone.

When I left college I studied with General Conger, who was afterwards head of G2 at Chaumont under General Pershing. He taught me much about war and gave me a deep respect for men who knew the art of war. It was from him that I learned what fearless and intelligent leadership meant to fighting men in the battlefield. It was he who after the Agadir affair in 1911 explained to me that when the Germans finished the Kiel Canal they would in all probability find some incident on which to make war, and begin their march toward the Mediterranean in order to build up a great central European empire.

When I asked Conger if he could name the controlling factors in late 1914 he thought for a minute and then said: "Yes, there are three: the French Army, the British Navy and the Allied Press. The Press will make clear the issues and that will eventually bring us into the war and ensure the defeat of the Central Powers."

General Marshall has told me that when he himself was a young man Conger was one of the best minds in the army.

After leaving college, and while I was still working with Conger, I spent two summers in the Shenandoah Valley studying Stonewall Jackson's campaigns. It was because Conger had convinced me that you could not make a good officer in less than seven years that I paid my own way to Paris and enlisted as a private in the American Expeditionary Force He did not approve of my judgment on that, but he liked my doing it.

Conger taught me the structure of modern war: the basic things that were needed to make war—manpower, the output of factories, raw materials, foodstuffs, science, and even psychological warfare, when back in those days few people had heard of psychological warfare. He was one of our greatest authorities on Prussian militarism.

Although Conger's teaching never made an amateur strategist of me it was because of what he taught me that, while living in Europe before this war, I became acutely aware of the malignance of Nazi political power and its military strength, and realised that the combination would once again threaten the peace of the world.

After Munich, when the Germans invaded Czechoslovakia, the British Government quickly recognised that it must adopt a war economy. The Johnson Act, which forbade borrowing from the United States by countries which had not repaid loans made in the last war, was still on the statute book of the United States. Mr. Chamberlain, then Prime Minister, took this legislation seriously and expected little help from the United States. He showed this when he failed to support Mr. Roosevelt's suggestion of January 12th, 1938, for the creation of a working committee of ten nations, representative of all regions of the world, to elaborate a clear-cut agenda to establish a basis for world agreement to maintain the peace. When the President secretly sounded out the Prime Minister, Mr. Chamberlain's reply was "in the nature of a douche of cold water."* The President had hoped that the proposal would lend impetus to the efforts of Great Britain and France to prevent any further deterioration in European affairs. He believed that, even if the major powers of Europe, including the Soviet Union, did not succeed in making any progress towards understanding, the United States would at least have obtained the support of all governments, except the Berlin-Rome Axis, in this effort to maintain world peace. Unfortunately the Chamberlain Cabinet was not the Churchill Cabinet.

Mr. Chamberlain later showed his prejudice against Russia when he refused to let Eden, or other ranking officials, attend the Moscow Conference in 1939.

But whether or not one agrees with Mr. Chamberlain's policy of appeasement, it is only fair to recognise that both he and Daladier had the support of many of their people when they met with Hitler and Mussolini and surrendered the Sudetenland to Germany in October of 1938.

The four powers, on Hitler's insistence, had excluded the representatives of both Czechoslovakia and Russia from the Munich Conference. The fatal weakness of that decision was not only in misjudging the intent and character of Hitler and Mussolini but also in the fact that the action taken broke the Protocols of Mutual Assistance under which France and Russia, and Russia and Czechoslovakia, had pledged themselves come to each other's aid in a war of defense. Munich

* Sumner Welles, *A Time for Decision*, p. 66.

wiped out the hope of an Eastern allied front. This put in jeopardy the possibility of holding an allied Western front against the powerful and prepared armies of the Axis. I so informed the President.

In writing of Mr. Chamberlain, it is interesting to note two paragraphs spoken by Winston Churchill to the British Parliament, when he paid a last tribute to this man with whose policies he had so fundamentally disagreed:

"It fell to Neville Chamberlain in one of the supreme crises of the world to be contradicted by events, to be disappointed in his hopes, and to be deceived and cheated by a wicked man. But what were these hopes in which he was disappointed? What were these wishes in which he was frustrated? What was that faith which was abused? They were surely among the most noble and benevolent instincts of the human heart— the love of peace, the pursuit of peace, even at great peril, and certainly to the utter disdain of popularity or clamour."

And again:

"When, contrary to all his hopes, beliefs and exertions, the war came upon him, and when, as he himself said, all that he had worked for was shattered, there was no man more resolved to pursue the unsought quarrel to the death."

These are revealing statements that show the heart and the untroubled fairness of the man who spoke them.

It was said by some that "Churchill enjoyed the war." No blacker lie was ever spoken. No one could have seen him, in the dark days of the war, as I did, and ever doubt his suffering or his caring. Someone asked Mrs. Churchill in 1936 if she thought her husband would ever be Prime Minister. Her answer was, "No, unless some great disaster were to sweep the country, and no one could wish for that."

I have been told that Mr. Chamberlain's military advisers forecast a three-years' war. With unusual skill he worked out the balance of annual tax contributions in relation to internal borrowings, but his external supply requirements which called for foreign-exchange payments were based not only on maintaining existing trade balances, but on a further expansion of foreign trade. The fallacy of this latter half of his program lay in the limited manpower at the command of the British. Sir William Beveridge, when I was talking with him in 1941, stated the relative position: "The British Commonwealth's strength in manpower is 75 million, the Germans have 80 million, the Italians 40 million and the two in combination control the supporting output of some 200 million allied or subjugated people."

When I was in Switzerland, one of our abler statisticians at the International Labor Office explained to me that when the Nazis came into power the total annual earnings of the German people ranged between 37 and 38 billion marks, but that after they had established their full employment scheme, which called for arbitrary assignment to work jobs and a longer work day, there was a gradual increase of total earnings and that production for civilian use was stabilised at approximately 42 billion, where it was pegged. This permitted a moderate increase in the standard of living, a fact which was noticeable in the beginnings of the Axis totalitarian regimes. It represented the meagre material advantage that went with the surrender of freedom to select jobs, of longer hours of work under compulsion. Eventually total annual earnings increased to over 80 billion marks per annum. All of the surplus was devoted to armaments, none for the further improvement of the general welfare. The barter system was introduced in order to ensure savings of foreign exchange and to permit accumulation of gold. An example of this was the purchase of the Bulgarian tobacco crop in exchange for furniture and other articles manufactured by German labor. The tobacco was not consumed in Germany but sold to Belgium for gold. Accumulated purchasing power in gold and foreign exchange was used to build up military strategic stock piles of materials which were not obtainable in Germany or Austria, or which were in short supply. This included wolfram, magnesium, copper and other war essentials, some less obvious, which could then be bought at reasonable prices on the world markets. Just prior to the war, and during the early periods of war before the Allied countries had developed their economic warfare organisations, there was considerable strategic counter-buying and bartering. The important factors in all this relate to the internal economy of a country and the necessity for foreign exchange.

In Britain, the accumulated savings in holdings of outside securities and gold balances, with the limited outside areas for borrowings, could not realise sufficient dollar purchasing power, or other foreign exchange, to finance the war; but on the other hand increasing foreign trade meant the continued absorption of millions of men and women engaged to supply goods for foreign markets and tied up merchant tonnage.

The heavy losses of merchant ships by submarines, raiders and enemy aircraft, and the extended patrol of the British Navy, with the resulting inability to protect convoys adequately, were felt early in the war. A consequence of these losses was the need for additional agricultural labor to increase domestic production because of the reduction of available tonnage for food imports.

The loss in the Dunkirk retreat of all British war material that had been shipped to France placed British Home Defense in a perilous position. It was then that the King asked his people to turn in their shotguns; I gave what aid I could to further the shipment of a million rifles from America to arm the Home Guard. It is interesting to remember that it was at this same time that one saw chalked up over the news-stands and everywhere the simple words, "There will always be an England." This undramatic resolution, this complete unwillingness to admit defeat which I saw in the people, was matched in their leaders.

The situation called for increased enlistments, increased output and a larger volume of imports of war materials which could only be purchased with monies acceptable to the country of manufacture.

Mr. Churchill had a complete grasp of the situation, and when he took over the government he enormously reduced the number of workers and the ships engaged in foreign commerce. He was too old a soldier not to know the need for manpower and material in maintaining armies in the field, and too good a sailor not to know what freeing ships from non-essential merchant trade would mean at that time. Nor was he unaware of the need for foreign exchange, but he " cast his bread upon the waters " and put his trust in Western democracy. It was a close decision, for at the most critical moment, when invasion still threatened, orders in the United States had to be cancelled because Britain had no more American dollars, and all supplies then coming from the United States were on a " cash and carry " basis. The sands of time were again running out.

It was "All aid short of war"—Roosevelt's Lend Lease answer—that met this desperate need and allowed the British to carry on their gallant fight against greater numbers, longer trained and better armed.

Lend Lease gave Britain the tools for defense and later enabled her to take the offensive, equipped and strong, but the force of Russian and United States might was needed to "finish the job."

The decision of Congress six months after Lend Lease to arm our merchant ships and permit them to enter combat zones was vital in maintaining the life lines of supplies from the American continent to combat areas.

A change of British policy which took place prior to this decision was of great importance in permitting a more orderly flow of goods and armaments under Lend Lease to Great Britain. The partial listing of British requirements for defense purposes had been forwarded to Washington from time to time in piecemeal lots. This was done for security reasons. It was feared that a total listing might get into enemy hands. If it did it would show up British shortages, which might open them to attack where they were least able to meet it. But this method did not permit coordination with our own wants or reasonable scheduling of raw material distribution and seriously interfered with factory production. Arthur Purvis, a Canadian, who had had charge of British purchases in the United States before Lend Lease became operative, and who had continued in Washington as head of the British Division of Supply, was fully aware of the situation. He therefore asked the British to prepare a master-list forecasting total needs over a given period. Purvis then persuaded the British Cabinet to support such a listing, with the understanding that it would go only to the President with the obligation on his part to limit its distribution. In order to complete these negotiations he had flown to London. I saw a good deal of him at the time and was able to give him assistance. When he left on his return to the United States I went out to the airfield to say goodbye to him and gave him a letter which I had prepared for the President. He flew to Prestwick to board a transatlantic plane. In the take-off his plane crashed and he was killed. The letter was picked up on the airfield and returned to me. But the plan was adopted. In the crowding of later events his service has passed almost unnoticed. He is one of the forgotten men whose contribution to the allied cause, in my judgment, has never been fully recognised.

Shortly after Lend Lease came into force I wrote the President about the British need for foreign exchange to hold the neutral countries, whether by trade or by loans, or by more indirect methods. These operations came under economic warfare. In this message I said:

"After the Lend Lease Act had been passed the question of taking over the British commitments in America, with particular emphasis on the resulting credit balances available to the British Treasury, was taken up with me, both by the Prime Minister and the Chancellor of the Exchequer. I reported these conversations in a previous cable forwarded to you and the Secretary of the Treasury, which included a letter to Under-Secretary Waley addressed to Ben Cohen (who was then attached to the Executive Office of the White House) summarising the situation from the British point of view. I stated the deep concern expressed here, but without making a personal recommendation. The matter has not since been brought up by either the Prime Minister or the Chancellor. The problem, however, will probably recur, as you cannot live here and not be aware of the growing reduction of national income due to a contraction of normal business, the transfer of the energies of the people to war production and war services, and the decline in the export trade. War strategy has been so closely related in these last few weeks to the situation in the Balkans and elsewhere that some flexibility in spending is necessary. It occurred to me that such situations will arise in which it might be simpler, as well as of advantage, for a country at war to be able to meet financial contingencies rapidly and from its own coffers. In the present circumstances shortage of funds might not only weaken Great Britain as a first line of defense, but be a sufficient threat to prompt us to find the money to meet a special situation that would be hard to explain to Congress in the time which the emergency allowed, and might be particularly embarrassing to handle without Congressional action with the Johnson Act still on the statute books. I do not want you to have to face that kind of headache. These, I realise, are probably Treasury matters. We are handicapped for the moment by the absence of anyone who is kept currently informed of the financial conversations at Washington. I understand that this situation is being given attention.

"In following up the point I have been making, Keynes,* who is associated with the Treasury, suggested that the situation was clouded at the end of the last war because it appeared that Great Britain had used our credits for other than war materials purchased in America. For that reason he thought it would be much better all around if we should confine the Lend Lease Act strictly to war materials but would be sufficiently generous in taking care of such materials to make

* Lord Keynes, British economist.

it possible for Britain to meet other obligations on her own responsibility."

Since I believed in the general thesis that Keynes had advanced, I began a series of conversations with the British Government in order to get agreement on the general policy of the use and the limiting of use of supplies sent to Great Britain under Lend Lease. The need of an open pronouncement by the British became apparent when charges were made in the United States that some of the materials that we were shipping were being used by British exporters in articles that were in competition with American goods in outside markets.

In order to clear the charges and to establish safeguards to protect both countries, I presented a note in early July to Sir John Anderson, then Lord President of the Council, in which I stated that we were concerned by reports that "The British were exporting steel manufactured into consumer goods items to South America and the United States," and that "other consumer goods requiring aluminum were being used for export trade." I asked for an investigation of the facts.

On receiving a reply, which I felt was incomplete, I asked for a more definite statement of policy.

On July 28th, I again pressed this matter at a meeting with Sir Kingsley Wood, Chancellor of the Exchequer, Lord Woolton, Minister of Food, and Lord Portal, Parliamentary Secretary to the Ministry of Supply. First we reached an agreement on policy which closely followed my original suggestions. A draft document was prepared and handed to me by Sir Kingsley Wood on July 30th. I forwarded it to the State Department in Washington. It received general approval. Although there were some persons opposed to the action I had taken, the President and Secretary Hull gave me complete support.

These negotiations culminated in the Eden White Paper, dated London, September 10th, 1941. This was forwarded to me with a covering letter. The following is an exact transcript of the agreement.

"(1) All materials which we obtain under the Lend Lease Act are required for the prosecution of the war effort. This principle governs all questions of the distribution and use of such goods, and His Majesty's Government have taken and will continue to take action to secure that these goods are not in any case diverted to the furtherance of private interests.

"*Export Policy*

" (2) Lend Lease materials sent to this country have not been used for export, and every effort will be made in the future to ensure that they are not used for export, subject to the principle that where complete physical segregation of Lend Lease materials is impracticable, domestic consumption of the material in question shall be at least equal to the amounts received under Lend Lease.

"(3) His Majesty's Government have not applied, and will not apply, any materials similar to those supplied under Lend Lease in such a way as to enable their exporters to enter new markets or to extend their export trade at the expense of the United States exporters. Owing to the need to devote all available capacity and manpower to war production, the United Kingdom export trade is restricted to the irreducible minimum necessary to supply or obtain materials essential to the war effort.

"(4) For some time past, exports from the United Kingdom

have been more and more confined to those essential (i) for the supply of vital requirements of overseas countries, particularly in the sterling Empire; (ii) for the acquisition of foreign exchange, particularly in the Western Hemisphere. His Majesty's Government have adopted the policy summarised below:

(i) No materials of a type the use of which is being restricted in the United States on the grounds of short supply and of which we obtain supplies from the United States, either by payment or on Lend Lease terms, will be used in exports with the exception of the following special cases:

(a) Material which is needed overseas in connection with supplies essential to the war effort for ourselves and our Allies, and which cannot be obtained from the United States.

(b) Small quantities of such materials needed as minor though essential components of exports which otherwise are composed of materials not in short supply in the United States.

(c) Repair parts for British machinery and plant now in use, and machinery and plant needed to complete installations now under construction, so long as they have already been contracted for. Steps have been taken to prevent the export (except to Empire and Allied territories) of such goods which do not come within the exceptions referred to in (a), (b) and (c) above.

(ii) Materials similar to those being provided under Lend Lease, which are not in short supply in the United States, will not be used for export in quantities greater than those which we ourselves produce or buy from any source.

"*Distribution in the United Kingdom of Lend Leased Goods*

"(5) The general principle followed in this matter is that

the remuneration received by the distributors, whatever the method of distribution, is controlled and will be no more than a fair return for the services rendered in the work of distribution. The arrangements rigorously exclude any opportunity for a speculative profit by private interests from dealing in Lend Leased goods. In most cases, Lend Leased supplies will be distributed through organisations acting as agents of His Majesty's Government in the strict sense of the term, and not as principals. Where for strong practical reasons this cannot be done a full explanation will be supplied to the United States Administration and their concurrence sought beforehand in any alternative arrangements proposed. The justification for retaining existing channels of distribution operating under strict Government control is that the creation of elaborate new organisation in their place would inevitably result in loss of efficiency and the wasteful use of manpower, and retard the war effort. In the distribution of Lend Leased goods there will be no discrimination against United States firms.

"(6) Food is a special case. Only some 5 or 6 per cent in tonnage of the total British food supply is coming from the United States and, without great practical complications, it would be impossible to have a separate system for the distribution of Lend Leased food. Food distribution is carried out in the United Kingdom by wholesalers, to whom the Government sells food as principals. In fact, the Ministry of Food has established a close control over all distributive margins, so that neither the wholesalers nor the retailers receive any greater remuneration than is adequate to cover the cost of the services performed. No food obtained on Lend Lease terms is or will be sold at uncontrolled prices. Thus the general arrangements as regards the issue of Lend Leased food fit into

His Majesty's Government's policy of stabilising the whole price level of foodstuffs, a policy to which the Government contributes £100 millions a year.

"(7) In some cases direct free distribution is practicable and will be adopted. For example, some milk products (including Lend Leased supplies from the United States) are distributed direct and free of charge to children and others in need through schools, clinics and hospitals. The distribution is undertaken by State agencies and the cost of the distribution is borne by the Government.

September 10, 1941."

This document is clear in itself. It represented an effort to get down on paper a statement of policy that was straight and sensible. It was also an attempt in general terms to define practice under that policy that would protect both the receiving country and the giving country. It was accepted by both countries.

There was a reverse side to Lend Lease which the imaginative minds that conceived it wrote into the document itself. It stems out of Article "B" of Section III, and was later formalised under the reciprocal aid arrangements contained in a letter dated September 3rd, 1942, addressed by Lord Halifax to Mr. Cordell Hull. In the conditions set down in this letter the United Kingdom undertook to "provide the United States or its armed forces with the following types of assistance as such reciprocal aid, when it is found that they can most effectively be procured in the United Kingdom or in the British Colonial Empire.

"(*a*) Military equipment, munitions and military and naval stores.

"(*b*) Other supplies, materials, facilities and services for the United States forces, except for the pay and allowances of such forces, administrative expenses, and such local purchases as its official establishments may make other than through the official establishments of the Government of the United Kingdom. . . .

"(c) Supplies, materials and services needed in the construction of military projects, tasks and similar capital works required for the common war effort in the United Kingdom or in the British Colonial Empire, except for the wages and salaries of United States citizens.

"(d) Supplies, materials and services needed in the construction of such military projects, tasks and capital works in territory other than the United Kingdom or the British Colonial Empire or territory of the United States to the extent that the United Kingdom or the British Colonial Empire is a more practicable source of supply than the United States or another of the United Nations."

It is easy to forget that in the passage of the Lend Lease measure the Congress stated that "This Act may be cited as 'An Act to promote the Defense of the United States.' "

When the war came to us we developed further the idea of mutual aid—the idea that each ally must put everything it had into a common pool regardless of whether one contribution was larger or smaller than another so long as every contribution was everything.

It would have been advantageous to the British after we became fighting allies to have reduced their manufacture of fighter planes and to have increased the building of long-distance bombers which they might later have converted into transport planes; to have built merchant ships which would later have been useful in their mercantile trading rather than build destroyers; and to have engaged a larger number of men in continuing their world cargo trade which in post-war years was essential to maintaining their standard of life. This, however, would not have been in the interest of the total war effort. We could produce in the United States bomber planes and merchant ships in mass production in greater numbers with fewer men and we needed to make large drafts on British manpower to prepare and support the invasion to France. It was because the British accepted this principle of mutual aid that they hoped there might be compensatory readjustments when peace came, based on a fair measure of mutual sacrifice.

In our concept of Lend Lease legislation we did not fail to look beyond the war in our desire to promote mutual trade and ensure full employment. In an agreement between the Governments of the United States of America and the United Kingdom, entered into on February 23rd, 1942,* we included a section which is referred to as Article 7 and which reads as follows:

"In the final determination of the benefits to be provided to the United States of America by the Government of the United Kingdom in return for aid furnished under the Act of Congress of 11th March, 1941, the terms and conditions thereof shall be such as not to burden commerce between the two countries, but to promote mutually advantageous economic relations between them and the betterment of world-wide economic relations. To that end, they shall include provision for agreed action by the United States of America and the United Kingdom, open to participation by all other countries of like mind, directed to the expansion, by appropriate international and domestic measures, of pro-

* Principles applying to Mutual Aid in the Prosecution of the War against Aggression.   Executive Agreement Series No. 241.

duction, employment, and the exchange and consumption of goods, which are the material foundations of the liberty and welfare of all peoples; to the elimination of all forms of discriminatory treatment in international commerce, and to the reduction of tariffs and other trade barriers; and, in general, to the attainment of all the economic objectives set forth in the Joint Declaration* made on the 12th August, 1941, by the President of the United States of America and the Prime Minister of the United Kingdom.

"At an early convenient date conversations shall be begun between the two Governments with a view to determining, in the light of governing economic conditions, the best means of attaining the above-stated objectives by their own agreed action and of seeking the agreed action of other like-minded Governments."

This article grew out of earlier conversations and exchanges between the two governments carried on both in London and in Washington. In order to support our position in Britain at that time I made a public address in Liverpool. It was in November 1941. Since these issues are still before us and we are in the process of remaking our economic policy, I would like to go back to the record and restate what I said then:

"There are two issues that face the free peoples of to-day—one is to see this war through and the other is to deal with the problem of reconstruction.

"When the war is over, we both will have to face an internal and an external reconstruction in our two countries which must involve broad changes of policy. Among the questions that will have to be dealt with are those of exchange, of trade, and with them of employment and the standard of living.

* Atlantic Charter. Dept. of State Bulletin. August 16, 1941, p. 125.

These are things which should be studied and understood now so that the mistakes following the last war can be avoided when this war is ended."

In the aftermath of the last war the League of Nations was unable to initiate rapid economic reconstruction. This resulted in a sharp return to economic nationalism. It was accentuated by a cycle of depression. The League of Nations could not open the broad highway of trade and free the exchange of goods. The nations set up tariff walls and other restrictive measures which stopped both goods and men crossing frontiers. This deepened the depression and increased unemployment. It laid the background and created conditions of unrest in impatient populaces which allowed minorities to take over governments. In Italy the loss of foreign exchange resulting from the cuts in immigration quotas to the Americas and the lack of raw materials opened the way for the blackshirts and Mussolini. In Germany, under over-weighted reparations, the slow painful processes of the development of democratic government were savagely tossed aside by the brown-shirts and Hitler. And in the overcrowded islands of Japan, liberal statesmen were assassinated and the military gangsters spilled over into Manchuria, which marked the beginning of World War II.

Mr. Cordell Hull has stated the American opposition to totalitarian economy with brevity and clarity, and at the same time laid down certain principles by which world economic reconstruction might be realised by free peoples:

"The main principles, as proven by experience, are few and simple:

"(1) Extreme nationalism must not again be permitted to express itself in excessive trade restrictions.

"(2) Nondiscrimination in international relations must be the rule, so that international trade may grow and prosper.

"(3) Raw material supplies must be available to all nations without discrimination.

"(4) International agreements regulating the supply of commodities must be so handled as to protect fully the interests of the consuming countries and their people.

"(5) The institutions and arrangements of international finance must be so set up that they lend aid to the essential enterprises and the continuous development of all countries, and permit the payment through processes of trade consonant with the welfare of all countries.

"(6) Measures taken to give effect to these principles must be freely open to every nation which desires a peaceful life in a world at peace and is willing to cooperate in maintaining that peace."

The acceptance of a one-world good-neighbor foreign policy not only affects security but will inevitably cut across individual concepts of domestic, economic and social policy. If the United Nations is to lift mankind it is not only necessary to redefine sovereignty in terms of cooperative security but also to make possible the expansion of essential activities to satisfy human wants. We hear much about Eastern blocs and Western blocs these days, but even in a split world it is possible to destroy unity in a Western bloc by a failure to grasp the rudimentary principles laid down in Article 7 of the Lend-Lease Agreement.

If, on the morn of the atomic age, we persist in once more hog-tying the diversity of talents and natural resources that can be contributed by all nations, we will assuredly plunge ourselves into mutual destruction, and turn our backs on the living possibility of a Golden Age.

IX

CONTACTS AND TRAVELS

THIS part of my story is made up of bits and pieces. It covers visits and meetings which are part of the ordinary duties expected of an Ambassador but, because of the times and the individuals concerned, took on an importance in themselves. I tried to make as many contacts as possible with all people everywhere and in all localities. I visited the university towns and the larger cities, and covered all those areas in which there had grown up traditional loyalties to particular sections of the country. This included the South of England and the port towns, the Midlands, the North Country, the North of Ireland, Wales and Scotland.

One of my visits was to Plymouth, where Lord Astor asked me to make the address at his fourth inauguration as Lord Mayor of Plymouth. I was glad to do this because of the brave resistance of the people of this great port town, and also because of the Pilgrim Fathers, as my home is in New England. I closed my remarks by quoting from Franklin K. Lane's great soliloquy as he stood before St. Gaudens' statue of Abraham Lincoln in Chicago: "It is to me all that America is, physically and spiritually. I look at those long arms and long legs, large hands and feet, and I think that they represent the physical strength of this country, its power and its youthful awkwardness. Then I look up at the head and see qualities which have made the American—the strong chin, the noble brow, those sober and steadfast eyes. They were the eyes of one who saw with sympathy and interpreted with common sense; they were the eyes of earnest idealism limited and checked by the possible and the practicable. They were the eyes of a truly humble spirit, whose ambition was not a love for power but a desire to be supremely useful. They were the eyes of compassion and mercy and a deep understanding. They saw far more than they looked at. They believed in far more than they saw. They loved men not for what they were but for what they might become. They were patient eyes, eyes that could wait and wait and live on in the faith that right would win. They were eyes which challenged the nobler things in men and brought out hidden largeness. They were humorous eyes that saw things in their true proportions and in their real relationships. They looked through cant and pretense and the great and little vanities of great and little men. They were the eyes of unflinching courage and an unfaltering faith rising out of a sincere dependence upon the Master of the Universe."

Through all the months I was stationed in London, before war came to us, I tried to help the British people see America through Lincoln's eyes.

The interest of the British in the United States was intense and the information available was totally inadequate to satisfy their desire for knowledge of our country. Most people had an unbalanced conception of American life which had been largely gleaned from moving pictures.

The Embassy was besieged by requests for literature from the youngest child to the oldest inhabitant. I realised the importance of satisfying this interest to meet the need of the moment and more particularly to develop a wider knowledge of the good in both countries.

One of the first things I did was to arrange through the Board of Education to discuss with teachers the study of American history in their schools—a subject which had not received serious attention in the British textbooks—and to persuade the American historian, Allan Nevins, who was at Oxford on a visiting professorship, to write a short history of the United States. This book had a wide circulation in Great Britain and was translated into French and also published in Switzerland.

The rigid economy in shipping space had greatly curtailed sending newspapers, magazines and books from the United States to Great Britain. The shortage of labor in the printing trade and the limited supply of paper reduced the size of the British newspapers to four pages. This further restricted the coverage of news from the United States. We tried to offset this in many ways. The British Broadcasting Corporation carried American news commentaries from Raymond Gram Swing and Elmer Davis in this early period. Both these men had a large listening public in Great Britain and were very helpful in explaining and interpreting American news. American foreign correspondents and visitors from the United States accepted the broadcasting facilities offered by the B.B.C., which also supplemented the curtailed information available through the press.

In transmitting news to the United States, a great service was contributed by our press correspondents and radio commentators. These men had schooled themselves in an understanding of international politics and military operations. They accepted discomforts and risked life cheerfully in their determined effort to keep the American people informed. "Ed" Murrow's broadcasts, "London Calling," became a kind of institution. Information given me at this time by William Shirer, Bill Stoneman, Ed Beattie, Wally Carroll, Bob Brunelle, Ray Daniel, Geoffrey Parsons, Bob Post, Ben Robertson, and Helen Kirkpatrick—and others like them—was invaluable to me in my official position and their reporting was an all-time credit to American journalism.

The British press has its head offices on Fleet Street within "the City." In the United States, because of its vast area, we have a local press or chain newspapers. In Great Britain, because it is physically possible to get daily delivery from London throughout the British Isles, printing and press ownership are concentrated in London, and even the provincial press is largely controlled from there. There are a few exceptions to this general rule in Scotland, Wales and Northern Ireland; and there are independent papers such as the *Manchester Guardian* and the *Yorkshire Post*. This concentration of press control in the British capital made it easier during the war to gather together the proprietors and editors of British newspapers than was possible in the United States. This was a convenience to the British Ministry of Information in maintaining constant contact with the press and in administering war censorship, although the Ministry of Information had its difficulties with the British service ministries. This was also true in our country after we got into war.

After I had been in Great Britain a short time I wrote the President that I had become aware of the wide gap between the British press and the American press. I explained to him that this was due to the fact that Britain was at war and we were not, that the British papers were under censorship and ours were not; also that the British press was telling the people that they were winning the war because of their courage and sacrifice, whereas our press was explaining that we were going a considerable way in winning the war because we were the arsenal and granary of democracy. Other things of course came into the picture, but the question of release of news appeared to me to be the bottleneck in the effort to build up mutual understanding. This had to do with the unwillingness of the military services to give out information which might be of advantage to the enemy, and I went on to say that the desire of the American people to be informed, in order that they might have a correct judgment on the situation, had at times been thwarted on the grounds of military security. I also told the President that I had been at considerable pains to explain the situation to the Prime Minister, the Foreign Office and all the Ministries concerned as I felt an informed American public opinion was a necessary protection to us and the British in our effort to help them. In a public address I made here, I said: "What America requires is not propaganda, but the facts. The case for Britain's need for convoys in my judgment is unanswerable, but the unwillingness to tell the whole story because of any assistance that might thereby be given to the enemy blocks the way to a clear comprehension of the true situation at home. This is understandable from the British point of view, but I believe that greater skill in selecting and releasing information would be a great help to us and of little damage to them."

Soon after my arrival, I went to Edinburgh at the invitation of Tom Johnston, Secretary of State for Scotland, to meet the Scottish editors. The meeting was at St. Andrew's House and we spent the afternoon in trying to make clear the position of the United States in its policy of "all aid short of war."

I made a similar trip to Northern Ireland where I met the government and the press. In London I had conferences with the editors of the provincial press. Always I was in contact with the editors of the London press.

I also made a point of meeting the men in British films as well as the American distributors, because not only the news reels but also the feature pictures played a very real part in the presentation of information. We tried to use all the media of communication to keep people accurately informed on the attitudes and activities in both countries. The American film industry, for example, was very helpful in presenting a true picture in Britain of the production of material under Lend Lease, and at the same time presenting in America a graphic story of the use and need of the armaments and foodstuffs which had been shipped into Britain under Lend Lease.

The radio in Great Britain is a non-profit-making organisation, under charter from the government. It is known as the B.B.C. and is governed by a non-political board, appointed by Parliament, with its headquarters in London. The management cooperated in trying to present to the British people a true picture of American policy. The day-to-day job of maintaining installations in the period of bombing presented a difficult engineering problem. This was further complicated because the transmission stations gave direction to the German raiders. The transfer of programs relayed from a station in a target area so as to permit uninterrupted reception without change of wavelength was an obstacle we never had to face in the United States. The reliability of B.B.C. news programs throughout the war was a continuing support to British morale.

Another essential service of communication was the Post Office, which controls the mail, the telegraph and the telephone services. In spite of heavy raid damage, these services were maintained throughout the war with depleted personnel and shortage of materials.

The telephone operators who worked at the exchanges during these trying times deserve praise for their steadiness and their courage. It was the responsibility of the Post Office to warn districts of imminent raids. Any telephone girl in the United States who has worked a switchboard during a fire, or who has been on duty during a hurricane, will appreciate what this meant.

Lord Leathers was Minister of Transport. His Ministry was responsible for meeting both civil and military needs. This included ocean shipping and transport by land and inland waterways. All through the blitz period it was combating damage to bombed marshalling yards, disruption to service because of cut railroad tracks and smashed harbors. Lord Leathers' long years in shipping and railroading allowed him to use his lifetime of experience in efficiently administering his government post. I always liked the respect that he and Bevin had for one another, for they had negotiated across the table for over twenty years—one representing transport management and the other transport workers. Fred Leathers was an operator, not a talker. It is said that when Churchill asked him to accept his Ministry he declined, saying that he had had no experience in politics and was not qualified to meet debating points as a member of the House of Commons. Churchill countered by saying that that problem was easily solved, that he would have him made a peer and they would appoint an Under-Secretary to represent the Ministry in the House of Commons.

This was done. Few men have accomplished more in government or so well deserved the thanks of the people whom they served.

There was a human side to the expansion in the overseas carrier trade. It had to do with the casualties and the hardships of merchant seamen. It has always been interesting to me that the Ladies' Garment Workers Union in the United States was the first to sense the need to provide a hostel and recreation center in London for Allied merchant seamen. Through their generosity we were able to establish the Merchant Navy Club in Rupert Street, which thousands of seamen of all nationalities used and enjoyed during their brief hours of shore leave.

One of the early trips I made outside of London was to Wales, which I visited with Mr. Clement Attlee, then Lord Privy Seal, and with the late Mr. Arthur Jenkins, who was his Parliamentary Private Secretary. I first met Mr. Attlee while I was in the International Labor Office long before the war. The British Conservative Government had invited me to visit the depressed areas and to make suggestions that might be useful in working out their unemployment problems. Mr. Attlee, who was then Leader of the Opposition, was deeply interested and most helpful. I was told then that his leadership of the Labour Party was due to the accident of compromise. Ernest Bevin was the outstanding head of the trade unionist movement, while Herbert Morrison, Chairman of the London County Council, was the unchallenged leader of the political elements within that group. It was said that if either of these two men attempted to force a show-down and take over from the other they would have split the Labour Party, and therefore both of them, in the interests of harmony and party solidarity, had agreed to Attlee's leadership. After I had known Attlee for some time I was reminded of Gilbert Chesterton's saying that "in compromise there is the ringing word 'promise'." He had absolute integrity. When he later became Deputy Prime Minister I am sure Mr. Churchill never had reason to give a thought to Attlee's scheming to succeed him, in spite of the fact that in the last war Lloyd George had taken advantage of the same position in a coalition government to take over from Asquith. Nor could Bevin or Morrison ever hope to supplant another man whose selflessness so completely placed him above intrigue.

I got interested in Attlee's past and found that he had attended a well known school in England, and that he had gone to University College, Oxford, where he had taken honors. I asked him once if he could give me a sketch of his life. No briefer or more modest autobiography could ever have been suggested by any public man:

"I went to East London 40 years ago. Ran a Boys' Club for 9 years before the First World War. Lived there for 15 years. Was Mayor of Stepney in 1919 and an alderman for seven years. Elected to Parliament for Limehouse Division in 1922 and six times since then without a break."

He forgot to mention that he had served for five years in the infantry and with the tanks in the First World War. There is a story that one of our Ambassadors who had not recognised him at some formal dinner asked him if he had been shooting recently in France. When Attlee replied quite simply, "Not since 1918," our representative missed the point!

On the trip to Wales with Attlee and Jenkins, we went to the mining and industrial districts and talked to the workers there. Crowds met us everywhere. People in Wales, as in every other section I visited in Britain, broke through police lines to ask me to thank those at home who had sent a child a sweater, or a woman a dress, or other useful things. There was sincere appreciation, which was almost pathetic in its intensity, for the help which was given in this time of great need.

We changed our routing on the trip in order to stop at a village where there had been a mine explosion that day. Several men had been killed and injured. A brother of one of the lost miners was chairman of the committee that came out to the edge of the town to meet us. I shall always remember his tall figure, his strength and quiet dignity. I was grateful that I had had the chance to spend a bit of my life working for safety in mines and to prevent silicosis. I respect men who go down into mines.

Later that day we visited another mining village which a short time before had been bombed by German raiders. Sixteen people had been killed, others injured and more than six hundred made homeless. I was told that the Civil Defence authorities in the area hurried rescue parties there, prepared to provide lunch and to arrange for billeting the homeless. By noon they found that only three people needed to be served lunch, and that it was necessary to find immediate billets for eleven out of the six hundred. The neighbors had cared for all the others and taken them into their homes, where they stayed for the duration of the war. This consideration of people for one another cut through class, broke down indifference, and built up comradeship and morale. We walked through the village. Small houses had been ruined and the debris from the buildings scattered untidily along the street. We had arrived in the late afternoon. The miners had just returned from the day shift in the pits. They and their wives gathered around us and, without ceremony, sang in Welsh their national songs.

These people are tuned to music and their lovely voices lifted us from the scene of smashed homes into a world of beauty of their own making.

My first invitation to attend manoeuvres came from General McNaughton, who commanded the Canadian forces in Great Britain. The General had served with distinction in the last war and was himself one of the ablest engineers in the Dominion. I went down to his Command in Surrey and saw for the first time flame throwers in action, and the demonstration of a new device invented by the General to clear minefields. All the British High Command were present, and the ranking United States officers who were stationed in the British Isles.

We stood on high ground watching tanks and flame throwers attack a series of trenches and machine gun-positions that were protected by walls of sandbags. I remember the danger to the men operating the flame throwers and the extent of the destruction of these temporary fortifications—even the grains of sand were melted by the flames. The demonstration was well done and carried through with precision, but it gave you a graphic picture of the horror of scientific warfare. The entire operation was reported to Washington by our military contingent.

Later, General Sir John Dill asked me to meet him in Glasgow. He took me the next day to Inverary to see the training of the first Commando troops who were under Admiral Sir Roger Keyes, the hero of the Zeebrugge raid in the First World War. We spent the day watching operations and inspecting new equipment. Many of the ideas which were developed here were used not only in coastal raids but also by the invasion forces in Africa, Italy, and later

in crossing the Channel to France. I made a detailed report to
the President on my observations.

About the same time, I went with Eden and Ambassador
Biddle to Scotland to see the Polish Army. A review was held
on our coming. We watched the mechanised units and the
mobile column of tanks, bren-gun carriers, motorised infantry,
artillery and anti-tank sections, which took over an hour to
pass the reviewing stand. These gallant fighters had rallied
around General Sikorski in Britain, making their way there
through Rumania, through Greece, Egypt, France and even
via Russia—to unite and form a courageous army determined
to take revenge upon the enemy who had overrun and pillaged
their country.

General Sikorski took the salute as the mechanised units
rolled by. He was a great patriot and was both Premier of the
Polish Government-in-Exile and Commander-in-Chief of their
Army. His death in an airplane accident in Gibraltar was one
of the great tragedies that left its mark in the upheavals that
followed in war-torn Poland.

On Independence Day, 1941, great attention was given to
the President's Fourth of July address. In it he explained that
the United States could not happily continue in an oasis in the
midst of a desert of dictatorships and that increasing numbers
of Americans were coming to believe that we must take our
full share in making certain that freedom would survive.

That same day I unveiled a memorial tablet to William
M. L. Fiske III, a gallant flyer who joined the R.A.F. at the
beginning of the war. He had been the first American pilot to
lose his life in this battle for freedom. The service was held in
the little chapel in the crypt of St. Paul's. We sang the Battle
Hymn of the Republic, not knowing then that when we were

to hear it again in that scarred and lovely cathedral it would be at a memorial service in memory of the Commander-in-Chief of the Armed Forces of the United States.

It takes great moral courage to join a foreign fighting force in another country, even though you believe in the cause for which that country is fighting. The first band of young men to join the British Army in England I met shortly after my arrival in Britain. They were five college boys—I called them "The Five Musketeers." They had joined the 60th Rifles. This was the British regiment that was ordered out of the American Colonies at the time of the Revolutionary War because its officers and men were in sympathy with our cause. The King is the Colonel of the regiment. In taking oath to the Colonel, these men did not lose their United States citizenship. It was Eden's old regiment. We used to stop together and see them doing their training in Westminster. When they were on leave in London they stayed in my flat. They were fearless men and they fought with great courage with the British army in the desert battles that ebbed and flowed over the Egyptian border to El Alamein and beyond. It would have been hard to find better representatives of a brave people. David Cox lost his life in the fighting round El Alamein, Jack Brister was killed just before the German surrender in North Africa, Charles Bolté lost a leg, Bill Durkee came out with a bullet through his knee and Heyward Cutting was twice wounded.

Gradually more fighters came over from the United States to join the R.A.F. It was not long before they were in sufficient numbers to form a squadron of their own—the Eagle Squadron. They asked me to be their guest of honor on the first Thanksgiving Day I spent in England and I thought, as I looked at their faces around the table, that America had reason to be very proud of them. Others were to follow. When war came to us, I was very happy to petition, at their request, that the Eagle Squadrons be accepted as units in the United States Army Air Force. This was done.

The first volunteer nurses from the United States who had come over to do hospital work were torpedoed on the way. With American help we had established the Churchill hospital at Oxford. No one can spend much time in the wards of military hospitals and ever want war.

You were always conscious of the presence of war, although all the meetings I attended did not directly bear on war. I remember that I was asked to meet with the Ministers of Labor of the Allied Governments in London. I had known them all when I was Director of the I.L.O. At this meeting they told what was happening to the workers of Occupied Europe. It was a tragic story. They told of their faith in ultimate victory and of their appreciation of the aid which was coming across the Atlantic. Many men who belonged to our group were absent because they were in occupied countries. One was Paal Berg, the Chief Justice of the Supreme Court of Norway, who had been Chairman of the Governing Body of the I.L.O. at the outbreak of war, and who later led the resistance movement in his country; Leon Jouhaux, leader of the French General Confederation of Labor, who was a hostage in German hands, and E. Kupers, President of the Federation of Dutch Trade Unions, who served as a key man in the underground resistance and who towards the end of the war was imprisoned and was listed for execution when saved by the liberation. Many of the men in the resistance movement on the Continent had come to the International Labor Conferences before the occupation.

As I told the American Federation of Labor when I spoke to them at their annual meeting in New Orleans the year before, "The tragedy of war has affected the national membership of the I.L.O. Individuals who have been associated with it have accepted the common lot of their countrymen and paid the price of their trade-union convictions even when this has meant imprisonment and death."

Ernest Bevin was present at this meeting of Allied Ministers of Labor and we talked of the labor conference which was to have been held in Geneva in June 1940, and the plans then under way to call it in the United States in the fall of 1941. Bevin had hoped to go over to the meeting, but instead it was agreed that Mr. Attlee would lead the British delegation and at the same time discuss with American labor leaders British wartime needs. It was at this meeting of the International Labor Organisation, held just before Pearl Harbor, that President Roosevelt met with this group of European leaders and broadcast to the millions who had been associated with the labor movement in Europe. His statement was re-broadcast from London in every language:

"I extend the hand of courage to the delegates of those labor organisations whose leaders are to-day languishing in concentration camps for having dared to stand up for the ideals without which no civilisation can live. Through you, delegates from those despoiled lands, the United States sends your people this message, 'You have not been forgotten; you will not be forgotten.' "

I wanted very much to get the story of the war across to the United States, told by plain people in simple language. I remember addressing the Executive Committee of the Working Women's Organisations. I told them that I wished I had the authority under reverse Lend Lease to lend them to America, and then added that the thing that counted most "in moving people at home to an understanding of all that this war means is genuineness, that in the last war the people who really moved America were not the orators, they were not the people with easy manners, they were the people who were thoroughly honest and believed in their cause; that if we could get a few 'homely' women, who would just speak the truth and be themselves, to tell the story of the defense of Great Britain, it would mean much to us." I was surprised by the response to this speech. Nearly all the audience wrote to me afterwards offering themselves for a tour of the United States! No one minded being "homely" in those days.

There was a different meeting of quite another character which took place in early October of the next year. I include it as it illustrates the compromise that must be made between a desire to be humane and the necessities of war.

Ambassador Myron Taylor, the President's Personal Representative to the Holy See, had come to London on a mission for the President to see the Prime Minister. He wanted to work out a formula to prevent the bombing of Rome. I called Mr. Churchill and he asked us both to dine with him that night in the Annex. It was one of the most absorbing evenings I spent in London because of the deep sincerity of those two men and the primary values under discussion. Each had a different cause to defend and yet they were common-purposed in their beliefs in the rights of free peoples, and each hated cruelty.

Mr. Taylor had just come from the Vatican where he had been in residence. Mr. Churchill had been living in bombed London. The British were fighting desperately in the Middle

East and the Allied invasion of North Africa was already planned. The bombing of Rome and the damaging of the Vatican would have offended Catholic opinion in the Western World. But if Rome was removed as a possible British target Mussolini might have been tempted to strike at Alexandria or Cairo, thereby endangering the success of the British armies before El Alamein.

No one who has seen Mr. Taylor could ever doubt his tenacity of purpose. He has the kindly simplicity that comes of a Quaker ancestry. He himself is an Episcopalian. He had won the friendship and confidence of the Pope, and had the respect of people of all denominations in the United States. What he said had great weight with Mr. Churchill, but the British Commonwealth was fighting for its life, and any limitation of action which might aid the enemy could well put in jeopardy the Mediterranean campaign.

Neither man would give way, but I believe great good came of this exchange of views. It was the most civilised conversation I have ever listened to which involved both spiritual considerations and the use of the destructive tools of war.

Taylor wanted to protect this great centre of spiritual influence, surrounded by the monuments of antiquity; Churchill was too steeped in the history of the past not to fully understand, but he felt he had a primary obligation to his troops in the field. It was not a conflict between these two men. It had to do with man's continuing failure to establish peace and freedom through the power of love, and every time that breaks down the only answer must always be an agonizing compromise between the spiritual and the temporal. Similar conflicts arise and pass unnoticed in day-to-day life, but are forever highlighted by the tragedies of war.

War with us was only a means to an end. We engaged in it to maintain our way of life. It was a defensive war. In the hearts of men there was a deep desire for world peace which called for world cooperation. While explaining the art of war, and pointing out the sacrifices made in war, I do not accept the inevitability of war. But I do believe that if civilisation is to advance to serve the ultimate good of mankind we must find ways and means of transferring the willingness to sacrifice on the battlefields to the peace front. We must find "the mora equivalents" of war. We need the generous and the brave and singleness of purpose if we are to unite the nations "to save succeeding generations from the scourge of war."*

* Preamble to the Charter of the United Nations.

X

INVASION OF RUSSIA
AND ATLANTIC CHARTER

IN May 1941 Harry Hopkins sent word to me that a clearer
picture on priority war material for the defense of Britain
was wanted in Washington. This called for a policy evaluation
by the British High Command on the military situation and
a statement of civil needs.

I had written the President, after being here a month, that
I wished he could see for himself the military map rooms and
charts and get a detailed and comprehensive view of the
British naval, army and air strategy. I realised that only men
who had spent a lifetime in studying the complicated field of
modern warfare could properly evaluate the total war picture.
Since, at that time, our own front lines of defense were the
navy patrols, I suggested to the President that he send a navy
man of the highest rank to London. I knew every facility
would be given him to study and report to the President on
the overall conduct of the war.

In order to cover this situation the President sent to London
in early May a naval mission under Admiral Ghormley and
an army mission under Major-General Chaney. Their arrival
assured the United States Joint Chiefs of Staff that they would be
currently informed, on the highest level, of British plans and
operations.

It was natural that, since we were not at war, there was
some hesitation in turning over to the United States military

attachés at the Embassy, on a day-by-day basis, complete operational information. The Prime Minister at this time reminded me, in limiting certain information asked for by our air attaché, that "only a handful of men in his own government were familiar with the complete overall strategy." The British, as I have already explained, were also slow in giving us full information on their lack of armaments, for if knowledge of weakness in British defense got into the press by inadvertence it could have reached the enemy and been used by them.

The question of security was rightly on the minds of those directing military affairs. The story of a conscientious American military observer in the Middle East illustrates the need for it. In reporting operations in that theater a weak code was used which was intercepted by the Germans. If this had not been quickly discovered by British Intelligence it might have led to serious consequences in the early battles in that area.

Before the arrival of the mission, however, the shortage in tanks and lack of armored divisions had become a pressing issue. The British had on paper three armored divisions, but there was, in fact, only sufficient equipment to put one fully-armored division in the field. We knew that the Germans had at least twenty armored divisions across the Channel. General Sir John Dill, who was keenly aware of the situation, asked that I meet him with the British Generals who were in command of the armored units to consider possible American production resources to overcome these deficiencies in the face of possible invasion. We spent an afternoon discussing the detail of tank production possibilities under Lend Lease. It was the first time I had heard a British suggestion of a joint Tank Board. There was no question of the need for new tank designs, but to work out a common effort involved the problem of our non-belligerency at the time. I had previously sent the President, on April 14th, a message covering this problem. Referring to the visit of a friend of his who had done tractor farming on a large scale in the West, I said, "The other day Campbell from Montana came in to see me. He had been visiting tank factories. He told me he found they had been making treads of malleable iron which he felt greatly lessened speed and would have a life of limited mileage. It gave me a lead, and I discussed the problem with an old British tank general. He had the same complaint, so I took the matter up with General Dill. He told me he could not over-emphasize the inefficiency of the British treads, that the Australian treads were no better, and that this had been one of the greatest handicaps in handling the British tanks in the Middle East. I understand that we have a hard rubber tread. . . . He also explained that their tanks were too slow. . . .

"I wanted you to know that there is an apparent difference of opinion between the Prime Minister and his staff on the subject of tank attack. The Prime Minister feels that the men should stand up against tank attacks, or let the tanks roll by and keep on fighting in the rear. The Germans did this in France. The Generals feel that the Prime Minister would stick it but that everybody wouldn't."

There were equally urgent problems in relation to aircraft and accessories and radar.

Another message to the President sums up requests for information and assistance which were necessary for the operation of planes of American manufacture that had been delivered to Great Britain, and also the means of conveying the latest developments and battle experience to airplane manufacturers in the United States. I had written that I thought British aircraft on the front was superior in combat to the American fighting planes being delivered from the United States. This was, unfortunately, true at that time. The reason for this I thought was the lag in transmitting technical information based on war experience to the manufacturers in the United States producing aircraft and accessories for Great Britain.

I explained that means had been provided by the Minister of Aircraft Production to speed up transmission of such information. This was complicated because new types and new developments in airplanes and accessories were of a highly secret nature and could not be sent direct to manufacturers in a neutral country. It had, therefore, been agreed after discussion with the Air Ministry, the Ministry of Aircraft Production and United States War Department representatives, that disclosure of lessons learned in combat and the complete interchange of plans for technical development could best be done by assigning carefully selected and qualified officers to absorb and transmit to the War Department technical and factual information in (1) aircraft and accessories, (2) armaments, (3) aircraft radio communications and navigational aids and (4) maintenance and repair.

At the same meeting, which was called at my request, I pressed for the pooling of British patents on the ground that Lend Lease aid coming from us, in my opinion, obligated the British Government and individual manufacturers to waive patent protection in the interest of defense. This was agreed to.

I also spent a morning with Lord Woolton, Minister of

Food. I had noticed that British children were beginning to look under-nourished; I felt concern for them.

Woolton was an effective administrator and before he joined the Coalition Government was one of the ablest merchandisers in Great Britain. His method of fairly sharing all available food was appreciated by the whole country. People could count on the ration quota—there were no gaps in its distribution, however small the amount. I always liked his gentleness in dealing with any problem that had to do with either the children or the mothers of Great Britain, and I also respected his disciplined efficiency. I was told that when he was made a peer many British housewives said he should have been canonised instead!

In my talk with him I learned that there were serious shortages of fats and proteins. This condition had been intensified by the decision to defend the Middle East. It made it necessary to take the refrigerator ships that were carrying fresh meat and other perishables from Argentina to Great Britain and use them to supply British forces in the Mediterranean theater.

Starches were also a problem. British agricultural policy at this time was determined by shipping. Up to 1939 only 25 per cent of British foodstuffs was produced in the British Isles and the great bulk of that was for animal consumption. The war forced a radical change. Before the end of hostilities these figures were reversed and the percentages of home-produced food for human consumption were enormously increased. The bulk tonnage in the pre-war shipments had been hard wheat for bread. The soft wheat produced in Great Britain was used in the main to feed livestock, a small portion being made into biscuits. The limited tonnage and the sinkings forced reduction in the hard-wheat shipments into the British Isles and compelled the planting of increased acreage of domestic wheat for bread. It took continued experimentation with soft wheat to produce a loaf with keeping qualities. Later it became necessary to reduce the wheat content by adding potato flour.

And yet in spite of this and the fact that the bread was darker in color, I felt that Woolton was correct in his reply to a woman who shouted at a meeting, "When are you going to give us back our white bread?" and he answered, "The bread you are eating to-day is a better loaf than you have ever had or are ever likely to have again." Unfortunately, because of dollar shortages in Britain, the loaf is not now as good as it was then.

There was a deeper concern that affected the overall picture. It was the serious losses of merchant ships and the shortage of protective ships for convoy. There had been an awareness of this in America from the beginning. The transfer of the destroyers was an open effort to protect British life lines. It was not sense to send munitions and foodstuffs produced by American labor, and paid for under Lend Lease, from America to the British Isles and have them sunk at sea. The advance of the patrols would relieve the pressure on the already over-extended British Navy. This was one more pressing problem that I had to take up with the President.

It was with all this in mind that I cabled him that I wanted to return for consultation. He asked me to come at once. I did so, arriving in Washington at the end of May.

Through inadvertence the date of my leaving London and the route to be taken were announced from the Embassy. I was flying from a British aerodrome to Lisbon and from there to New York via the Azores and Bermuda. The Germans picked up the information and sent out a plane to intercept us on the first leg of the journey, but the British had provided fighter escort planes and the German was shot down.

When I reached Lisbon I found that the United States Minister was ill, and that there was no adequate provision at the Legation to safeguard the confidential papers I was carrying from the Prime Minister to the President. I therefore went on to the British Embassy, where they were put in a safe, under guard. I spent the night myself at the Avis Hotel. The next day I collected my papers and went on to the United States by a Pan-American plane. Immediately on arriving in New York I telephoned Secretary Hull and learned from him that the President was at Hyde Park. I called him there and he asked me to go on to Washington the next day and stay with him at the White House. In New York I stopped, as was my custom, at the Roosevelt Hotel. After I had been there six hours a German agent, who was operating from the Hungarian Legation, took a room next to mine. I was immediately informed of this by the F.B.I. After that J. Edgar Hoover assigned one of his men to protect my papers. He stayed with me until my return to Great Britain.

I flew on to Washington and, after calling on Secretary Hull, went on to the White House. The President realised that staying there enabled me to talk with him and his advisers without the pressure of fixed appointments. I tried to give the President a clear picture of British resistance. He was intensely interested in every phase of it, and asked that I take up particular problems with the members of the Cabinet and the Chiefs of Staff.

I called on Secretary Morgenthau at the Treasury and we discussed at great length the question of dollar balances which was of concern to both countries. His quick perception of the British foreign-exchange position and its vital importance in prosecuting the war prompted him to give every assistance possible within the limits of the authority delegated to him. I was interested afterwards to note that, when we were attacked at Pearl Harbor, the Treasury Department was effectively organised to meet immediate war conditions.

One evening I went on a boat trip down the Potomac with Secretary Knox. We talked of old days in New Hampshire. We had had our political differences then, but no one could have been more cooperative in helping me in my effort to work closely with the United States Navy Command in London.

Later I saw Secretary of War Stimson. I never talked with him or with Secretary Hull without a deep sense of gratitude for all that they had done, not only in this war, but over long years of devoted service. Accumulated experience had given them the gift of wisdom.

There was another strength that was apparent to me even on this brief but crowded visit. It was what you might call the second line of defense in the War and Navy Departments; the under-secretaries and assistant secretaries and their good relationship with one another. They had been appointed without regard to politics. Their efficiency, integrity and loyalty to their common job prevented chiselling or dissensions, and their drive and industry gave you a lift when you went into their offices. On that journey I saw Robert P. Patterson Under-Secretary of War; James Forrestal, Under-Secretary of the Navy; Jack McCloy, Assistant Secretary of War, and Bob Lovett,* Assistant Secretary of War for Air. The first

* This was written before Robert A. Lovett was named Under-Secretary of State.

three have since been named for high office. In honoring them I hope Bob Lovett's great service to the men who flew in the war will not be forgotten—will always be remembered.

In combination, and with the support of the Truman Committee, these men played a large part in making this the cleanest war on the "contract front" that has been fought by the United States.

I reported to General Marshall, Admiral Stark and General Arnold, and gave each of them the complete story of the current war situation, as I saw it.

When I called on Secretary Wickard at the Department of Agriculture he insisted on my eating many different kinds of dehydrated foods with which he was experimenting at the time. These experiments in the end made possible great savings in tonnage and the export of more nutritious foods to Britain. In the beginning under Lend Lease we were supplying 6 per cent in tonnage of British food consumption, with an approximate 6 per cent food value. After a short time, while keeping within the 6 per cent tonnage limit, we were able to increase the food value to 25 per cent.

One day in Harry Hopkins' room we discussed food problems with Vice-President Wallace, Secretary Wickard and a group of experts from the Department of Agriculture. It was at this meeting that it was decided to increase the price of surplus milk so that more would be available for conversion into dried milk for Great Britain. This enabled Lord Woolton later to release larger quantities of whole milk to British children. The production of dried milk, like canning, had been a seasonal industry. The manufacturers took advantage of the large milk surpluses in the summer months. We hoped that a higher price would encourage farmers to feed more grain and bring up the annual milk production sufficiently to maintain a surplus for an all-the-year-round dried-milk industry. Up to that time dried milk had been largely for animal use and it was necessary to improve its quality for human consumption. This also was done and a plan worked out to improve and enlarge the plants manufacturing dried milk.

In discussing fats and meat we were very conscious of the fact that although it was possible to build a factory in three months it took a four months' cycle to produce a pig, whatever you did, and even longer to fatten it for slaughter. There was already a serious shortage of pork and bacon. In order to meet this emergency it was decided to raise the price of heavy hogs to induce farmers again to feed more grain and so to produce the greatest bulk in the shortest possible time.

All this required financing, which I was told could be arranged through the Federal Loan Agency. It also called for understanding by the American farmers in order to enlist their cooperation. Before leaving the conference, Henry Wallace suggested that I talk with some of the Senators. I wanted very much to do this. Harry Hopkins, however, felt strongly that I should limit my audience to a few members, since much of the information they would want had been given to me by the British Government with the understanding that it would be protected. Knowledge of British shortages and weaknesses could reach the enemy if the information I gave got into public debate.

I went on a Thursday afternoon to the Vice-Presidential Chambers and there met Vice-President Wallace and four Senators. We talked together for two hours or more and it was understood that there would be no public report of these conversations. On Sunday I flew to New York for the weekend and was greeted at two a.m. at the airport by the morning papers. One headline read, "Winant Reports Britain Thinks Victory Certain," another "British Position Extremely Grave But Not Disastrous, Winant Says." Both papers went on to report my conversation with the Senators, in garbled form. One said, for example, that "the British believe they have air superiority over the channel and invasion ports of Occupied France—a conclusion supported by a sharp decline in daylight bombings and fewer successful night raids by the Nazis in recent weeks." The other mentioned the protection of Channel ports in the "Kentish corner," but expressed alarm for the Northern and "back door" ports. My dismay on seeing these reports returns to me even now when I re-read the clippings. I could only hope that the conflicting nature of the articles might in some measure confuse the enemy, but I could draw little consolation from this thought. Later I gave a press interview which I hoped might correct any damage which had been done.

In the interview I emphasised the fact that "it is not the paid agent that is the great danger, but the confusion of honest people who unwittingly aid the enemy." My efforts to clear this picture were greatly helped by the President in the press conference he held before these unauthorised articles appeared. He explained that he had detailed information covering the propaganda methods that were being used by the Germans in their effort to obtain support in the United States. He added that the orders which had been issued to the Nazi and Fascist agents in the United States and their supporters asked them to play up, at that moment, the two following points: one, that

Germany had no thought at all of ever doing anything against the United States or any country in the Western Hemisphere; and two, that they had sent word out to take advantage of my arrival in the country from London by falsely reporting that I had brought back a statement that Great Britain's condition was desperate and that the United Kingdom was considering peace terms. The President stated that he thought there were not many dupes in America who would still be fooled by German assurances, and that Ambassador Winant had not brought back any information that Britain was considering peace terms, "not even a tenth cousin of peace proposals." These remarks were made in answer to newspaper reports that appeared immediately after my arrival. The President's statement served also to awaken Americans to the fact that Nazi agents were operating in the United States.

I returned to Washington for further interviews and started my journey back to England the following weekend. I went first by air to New York and left late in the evening by car for Deerfield, Mass. There, Dr. Boyden, the Head of Deerfield Academy, was kind enough to wait up for me until the early hours of the morning, so that I could have half an hour's talk with my two sons who were in the school and whom I had not seen for a long time. I arrived at our home in Concord, New Hampshire, for an early breakfast and, immediately after, flew to Montreal, and from there to Newfoundland. Before we reached Gander, however, the Captain came back to tell me that there was something wrong with one of the engines and asked if I could stop overnight. When I told him I should press on, he said he would idle the engines on landing, and have an engineer come out at once to locate the trouble. I have often thought since how my urgent request, and my need to get back to England, contributed to an accident I can never forget. A young soldier from Montreal, doing guard duty outside the hangar when we landed, stepped into one of our propellers in the darkness and was cut to pieces.

When I arrived in Prestwick I was given a special plane so that I was able to reach Chequers the morning of Friday, June 20th.

I made the following report to the Prime Minister. The President had agreed to three things: (1) the further extension of the area of patrols in the Atlantic which released more British protective shipping for other areas; (2) the occupation of Iceland as a defense outpost which would place United States troops nearer Great Britain in case of invasion (though the actual occupation was delayed because of statutory limitations on the use of State Militia and Selective Service units outside of United States territory which was not fully realised at the time the decision was made);* and (3) in the event that the Germans struck at Russia the President promised an immediate supporting statement following any announcement the Prime Minister might make welcoming Russia as an ally.

At Chequers I found Mr. Eden, Lord Cranborne and Lord Beaverbrook, and also Sir Stafford Cripps, the British Ambassador to Russia, who had come down to ask to resign on grounds of ill-health. Mr. Churchill had agreed to accept his resignation. When I talked with Sir Stafford I gathered that he thought there was no possibility of Russia attacking Germany.

British Intelligence had shown, even before I left for America, that Germany would, in all probability, attack

* These first two actions were publicly announced by the President on July 7, 1941.

Russia. This information had been passed on to the Russians but was largely discredited by them as British wishful thinking. It was because of this expected attack that I had been anxious to hurry my return trip to Great Britain. As it was I had only just made it, for in the early hours of Sunday morning, June 22nd, news came through that Germany had attacked Russia on a fifteen-hundred-mile front stretching from Finland to the Black Sea.

Mr. Churchill asked Sir Stafford Cripps to return immediately to Russia, which he did. The Prime Minister himself wrote the now famous speech which he broadcast that evening. In this he attacked Communism but promised Russia and the Russian people the full support of Britain. His closing words were: "The Russian danger is therefore our danger and the danger of the United States, just as the cause of any Russian fighting for his hearth and home is the cause of free men and free peoples in every quarter of the globe. Let us learn the lessons already taught by such cruel experience. Let us redouble our exertions, strike with united strength while life and power remain."

Immediately following this, Sumner Welles, acting for the President, made the supporting statement which had been promised.

This last act of Nazi aggression meant an Eastern Front, divided German forces, and that this vast country with its 160 million people would be fighting on the side of the Western Allies.

I remember that evening Churchill stated his faith in their power of resistance. General Sir John Dill, who was with us, was less sure. In trying to measure the sense of Hitler's drive to the East I could not myself but think of Napoleon. I remembered the snows and the winter winds that destroyed his great army. A child's verse of Kipling's came to my mind from his "A St. Helena's Lullaby" :

"How far is St. Helena from the Beresina ice?
An ill way—a chill way—the ice begins to crack.
But not so far for gentlemen who never took advice
(When you can't go forward, you must e'en come back!)"

The day following the German attack on Russia I had a long talk with Ivan Maisky, Russian Ambassador to Great Britain. All through the difficult days when he was in residence in London and his country compromised by its mutual non-aggression pact with Germany, I made a point of seeing him and continuing the friendly contact we had established in earlier days in Geneva. I hope that the ability with which he represented his country in that earlier period, and later before war came to them, will always be recognised.

I also spent some time with Mr. Eden, because the entry of Russia into the war necessitated a radical reorientation of the British position and indirectly affected us. In Parliament the next day, he reported on the Russian acceptance of the British offer of aid and announced that British military and economic missions would leave shortly for Moscow. He closed on a note of gratitude to the United States. He said he was glad to report that I had been greatly impressed on my visit home by the immense production effort in the United States, and went on to say, "the past few hours have brought fresh indications and fresh assurances of the continued increasing support of our American friends."

In late July, Harry Hopkins came over to discuss Lend Lease

supplies directly with the Prime Minister. He was invited to meet with the British Cabinet and, on the evening of July 27th, he made a radio address to the British people. The final arrangements for the Atlantic Conference were made while he was here. He planned to return to Washington and came to my office in the Embassy to go over with me the details of his conversations with British officials. When we had finished I told him that we had to do something for Russia. He answered that he realised the need but that we had no authority to move. I said that even a generous gesture would mean something in the desperate fight that was being carried on with such gallantry and sacrifice on the Eastern Front. I asked him if he thought it would help if the President would allow me to fly to Russia in order to carry some message of encouragement. He said he thought it would, and then, after a moment of silence, he said, "What would you think of my going from here?" I said that it would mean much more because I was certain that Stalin knew of his relationship with the President, and the part he had played in getting Lend Lease materials to Great Britain. We worked out together a telegram to the President. In a very short time the reply came back, "Go ahead."

Everybody moved at once to get him off, and the British arranged for a plane. He asked me to take care of his Russian visa. I called Maisky, who was in the country, and he started at once for London. It was usual at that time to clear all permissions for entry into Russia through Moscow, but the Ambassador sensed the value of this visit and wrote in the permission in his own handwriting. He told me this was unique in Russian visas.

I drove to the railway station to catch Harry before he left for his airfield in Scotland. I remember running through the station and up the platform. His train had already started and Harry was leaning out of the window, still hoping that I would arrive. I handed him the passport and wished him luck. I still believe that his journey was a turning-point in the war. No one could have done a better job.

The visit was followed two months later by the Beaverbrook-Harriman mission to work out Lend Lease agreements with Russia. Even laymen knew that putting the Russian army on wheels and supplying certain other deficiencies would offset the frightful losses they had suffered, and that they could then close their ranks and drive back the invader. We had the tools, and Lend Lease was the vehicle that permitted transfer from the greatest productive industrial area in the world to the largest land army that faced German invasion.

On Harry's return he went directly to Scapa Flow and boarded H.M.S. *Prince of Wales.* I flew up to Scotland the next day and motored to a pier, where I was picked up by a tender. It was cold and raining and a low fog hung over the Flow. I shall never forget the somberness of the scene, with the grey ships of the British Home Fleet barely visible in the mist, and the warm and friendly welcome when we got on board, with Harry there safe back from his flight to Russia. He was tired and ill. In the hurry of getting off to Moscow he had failed to take the medicines and injections which in those days kept him alive. I talked with Admiral of the Fleet Sir John Tovey, and the ship's doctor. They promised that they would take the best of care of him, and they did.

We dined together that evening. Harry told us about his meeting with Stalin, and was the life of the party until we pressed him to go to bed.

We postponed our private talk until morning, but when I went into his cabin, he was still asleep. He looked so utterly worn out I could not bear to wake him. In the end I left him a long letter and started back to London, where I had to be that evening. The Prime Minister went on board the same afternoon and they started together on their journey to Placentia Bay for the Atlantic Conference.

The story of the Atlantic Charter has been told by those who attended that meeting. It was an historic occasion. It marked out the foundation on which international action has been built. One of the ablest participants has described it as the "beacon which the English-speaking democracies held aloft to the peoples struggling for liberty to light them forward to peace, to human progress and to a free world."*

It brought together for the first time the Joint Chiefs of Staff of Great Britain and the United States. It made easy the transition into a Combined Chiefs of Staff. With Russia's aid on the Eastern Front it marked the beginning of the end of the Axis powers.

I shall always remember Attlee's quiet voice reading the Charter on the B.B.C. on the night of August 14th. There were some in the British Isles who were disappointed that the meeting of the President and the Prime Minister did not lead to a declaration of war by the United States, but no thoughtful person who listened to that Declaration could have failed to realise that the spiritual forces of a war-torn world lived on, and in the end would prevail.

It has always seemed to me fair to put on record the fact that not only was the British Cabinet in London given an opportunity by the Prime Minister to approve of the action

* Sumner Welles, *Where Are We Heading?*, p. 3.

taken, but that it was also from London that the suggestion of the Fifth Article was made which states the "desire to bring about the fullest collaboration between all nations in the economic field with the object of securing, for all, improved labor standards, economic advancement and social security."

It was accepted by the participants aboard the cruiser *Augusta* and incorporated into the Charter.

XI

BRITISH HOME FRONT

War today is not a conflict between armed forces drawing on a home base—it is a death fight between entire nations, each reaching out to destroy the manpower and the resources of the other. We saw that in bombed Britain, in the destruction of Germany and, in the end, in the obliteration of Hiroshima. There were fewer men killed in battle in this war than in the last, but more women and children. Each successive war reaches deeper into the civil population and necessitates the organisation of home fronts as well as battle fronts. We were spared attack on our home base this last war. No one can hope that this will be true if war comes again. I have, therefore, described in detail the organisation of the civil population in Great Britain.

Because their house was in order, they were not only able to hold at bay the enemy which had overrun Europe, they were able, with the aid we sent them, to build a firm springboard for us to cross the Channel with them and smash the Axis armies on the Western Front. We did not find a war-weary people, but a taut, disciplined, alert nation restless to be at the enemy.

It is not enough for those who love peace to talk peace. A lover of peace must understand war—its causes and its course. It is not enough to hope. We must also work desperately on practical measures that sometimes seem far short of our dreams.

Always the urgency of the military situation was reflected in the measures taken on the British Home Front. I tried, in my reports, to give some idea of the inter-relationships between the various measures adopted in regard to labor, taxation, finance, manufacturing industries and service occupation; as well as food, nutrition and social welfare.

But it is impossible to describe the Home Front without thinking in terms of people and organisation. The coordination of the civil activities came under Sir John Anderson, member of the War Cabinet and Lord President of the Council. He was an Independent Member elected to Parliament by the Scottish Universities. He had spent his life as a British civil servant, and had great gifts as an administrator. His ability in integrating the skill of the expert, whether scientist, engineer or economist, without disturbing the efficiency of routine controls, permitted the maximum contribution by the expert, and the full author-itative drive of officials responsible for purely administrative activities. There was no duplication or waste of brains or energy in the functioning of his overall planning. Mr. Churchill referred to him as the "Home Front Prime Minister." He was tough and hard working, patient and sagacious. Nor did he give the impression of being endowed with more than average ability—a nice trait in a man who can afford it.

In the late summer of 1941 the British had been fighting two years, the enemy was only twenty miles from their shores, they were constantly subjected to air attack, their manpower was limited, and the larger part of their population concentrated within a small area. These factors influenced the attitudes of all people toward government. Individual sacrifices were com-mensurate with the need. The government assumed a more rigorous direction and control of its citizens than any other government in the history of Great Britain. The fact that the existence of the country was at stake was responsible for the general acceptance to obey the drastic regimentation which was imposed in order to mobilize the nation's full resources.

The greatest shortage in Britain was manpower, with only 45,000,000 people to draw on. The registration and allocation of men and women to the services and to industry and agriculture were the responsibility of Ernest Bevin. When Churchill became Prime Minister, he asked Bevin, then the outstanding leader of the trade-union movement, to join the Coalition Cabinet as Minister of Labour and National Service. The Ministry itself has a far more inclusive jurisdiction than the Department of Labor in the United States.

I first met Bevin in Geneva when we were trying to get the rights of merchant seamen recognised, and by international agreement eliminate competition based on unequal labor costs, and at the same time provide fair standards for seamen.

You could not sit in the same conference room with Bevin without recognising his drive and capacity. I shall always remember a day in June 1940 when I had flown over from Geneva to London. It was the time of Dunkirk. Just before returning, I had stopped at the Foreign Office to see Lord Halifax, who was then Foreign Secretary. He was out, so I called on "Rab" Butler, the Under-Secretary. While we were talking a messenger came in to say that Italy had just declared war on Great Britain. "Rab" excused himself to meet a group of officials in order to reorientate Britain's foreign position to meet this shift of events. I explained to him that I was on my way to keep an appointment with Bevin and he asked me if I would explain the situation to him.

I crossed Whitehall to the Labour building and was shown at once into Bevin's office. He was sitting in a chair that was not built for him, a great hulk of a man. He called out to me as I passed through the door and, before I had a chance to speak, began explaining the pressures and problems that were piling up because of the fall of France. I broke in after a minute or two and gave him Butler's message of Italy's declaration of war. He went back in his chair for a moment and then seemed to gather all his energies, and came forward across the desk. He had already begun to plan to meet this new emergency. Both he and Churchill had the same fighting stamina for meeting reverses head on and standing up to the challenge of ill-fortune. We worked out a plan for transferring the International Labor Office from Geneva to Canada, and then he left me to go to the Cabinet Room.*

It was the long hard years of faithful service in the cause of labor that allowed him to put so heavy a burden on the workers of Great Britain. Trevor Evans, in writing of him, says: "Many prophesied in those war years that when the war ended this would be remembered against him. It was forecast that he would suffer politically for having disintegrated homes and separated families. Bevin himself was told of this many times. He never shared such forebodings. I remember him saying one evening, when this point was brought up to him: 'Not on your life. I am not imposing dictation from above on an unwilling people. All I am doing is putting the form to what people want. We are all in this war, and the people who know it best of all are those who are now being directed to jobs all over the place.'"

* I want to interrupt here to pay a tribute to Mackenzie King, who made it possible to transfer the International Labor Office to Canada where it was in a position to render effective aid in the war years.

The record of what Great Britain achieved in handling her domestic problems is, I think, impressive in four ways. First, it was a judicious blending of careful advance planning and quick adaptation to meet new situations as they arose. Second, there was a remarkable coherence and consistency about the plans as they related to different occupations. And in a country as small and homogeneous as Great Britain it was possible to see the pattern plainly. Third, the workers themselves voluntarily suspended for the duration of the war many of their fully accepted rights of collective bargaining. The mobilisation of British resources was obtained, in large measure, by the full and careful consultation by the government of the trade unions as well as the employers' organisations at every stage. Representatives of the workers and the employers participated throughout in the formulation of the wartime controls and helped in their application. Fourth, at the end of the war 42 per cent of Britain's employed population was engaged on war production or was serving in the forces. No other country can show a higher degree of mobilisation.

Britain had made a costly mistake by starting the 1914-18 war with voluntary recruitment, with the result that large numbers of skilled workers indispensable to the munitions industry were diverted into the armed forces. This mistake was not repeated. In 1939, before the war began, a schedule of reserved occupations was drawn up which provided for the temporary exemption from military service of men of certain ages in whole occupational blocks. The exemption applied whether the men were employed or unemployed.

The schedule was drawn up on a rough-and-ready basis and gave a wide margin of protection to strategic industries and occupations. But as the war developed and the need for men in the forces increased, the process of exempting men by occupational blocks was gradually modified into a finer instrument, and individual cases were taken up to determine the indispensability of particular men to war production.

This was combined with a further provision whereby men in vital war plants called "protected establishments" were exempted from service at a lower age than men in less necessary establishments. For example, an electrician in a vital plant would be exempted from service if he was twenty years old or more, but in a less essential industry he would not be exempted unless he was thirty or over. This scheme was intended not only to produce more men for the forces but also to encourage men with skills useful to war production to move into plants doing the most vital types of war work. It also dried up the non-essential industries by removing the manpower.

As the war continued the exempting gradually narrowed down in response to changed military and war production needs. Dependency did not enter into account. The indispensability of the man or woman in his or her work became the basic criterion for deferment. Except for a very few types of workers, men exempted from military service were allowed to volunteer into the services with permission from an Employment Exchange, and any person could volunteer at any time for a permanent career with the regular military establishments. At intervals of time, as an emergency device, all volunteering was stopped for men in certain occupations until the Ministry of Labour could revaluate a particular situation. There was no permanent exemption from military service. Each man's and each woman's case was subject to reconsideration. His or her exemption was temporary only.

So much for the system which enabled the forces to get the men they needed. There was another and equally important side to the manpower problem, namely the mobilization of the manpower of the country for the munitions industries.

A part of this was the process of squeezing out labor from the non-essential industries. For this purpose, and also to conserve factory space and materials, Great Britain put through a very thorough program known as the "concentration of industry." There were many industries in Great Britain whose scale of production could be greatly reduced without injury to the war effort. These industries were forced, as the war went on, to give up a large proportion of their labor to the munitions and other war industries. It was clearly less economical to allow all the factories to continue working each at, say, half their strength than it would be to close down half the factories altogether and concentrate the production in the other half. In this way non-essential industries were made to do with fewer workers.

A careful scheme for the concentration of essential industries was also worked out. The first step was for the Board of Trade to settle the reduced level at which a particular industry would be required to work in war. The next step was to decide how the concentration should be carried out. A very large firm would consolidate its activities by shutting up several branches or factories and concentrate work in the remainder. In other cases groups of firms agreed that one of them should produce to the specifications of the others, while each could continue to market the goods under its own trade name. Other arrangements were made where the circumstances required it.

The sum total was a far greater saving of manpower and

factory space for war industries than could otherwise have been achieved and non-essential products were eliminated.

This process of concentration of industries is only one example of the immense redistribution of labor that went on throughout Great Britain. Another instance was the building industry. At the beginning of the war Great Britain had over 1,300,000 men in the building and the constructional engineering industries. For a year or so there was a great deal of activity in building war factories, camps, aerodromes and constructing other military installations. But as these projects were completed more and more men were taken out of the building industry which, by the middle of 1944, was limited to only 600,000 men.

Another instance was in the distributing trades, which dropped from about 1,900,000 men and 1,000,000 women in 1939 to 970,000 men and 960,000 women in the middle of 1944. This great saving of labor was, of course, paid for in part by the housewives of Britain, who had to spend longer time waiting in queues. There were also fewer goods to buy.

Side by side with this process of drawing labor out of the less essential industries for the fighting services and munitions was the process of substituting women for men. The total number of women in industry in 1939 was about 4,800,000. This figure rose to 6,600,000 in the middle of 1944, at which date there were also more than half a million women in the fighting forces as well as those in Civil Defence.

The organisation for bringing about these sweeping changes in the distribution of Great Britain's manpower and womanpower was developed gradually and by stages. The first step was the announcement that the engagement of workers in a number of occupations had to be made through the Employment Exchanges. New machinery was developed to augment the Exchanges and to help them with their wartime duties, but this machinery was all linked closely with the Employment Exchanges and with the supply departments.

When the ground had been sufficiently prepared, and when employers and workers were conscious of the need for more control and ready to cooperate to meet it, the Essential Work Orders were adopted. This measure prevented undesirable movements of labor and facilitated those which were useful.

The purpose of the Essential Work Orders was to prevent employers from dismissing workers, and workers from leaving their jobs, without the consent of a National Service Officer (a Ministry of Labour official). It could be applied to any industry or any firm at the discretion of the Minister of Labour.

Almost all land and sea transport, mining, building, war manufacturing and essential civilian plants, and agriculture in Scotland, were covered by these orders. Their importance in effectively placing war workers cannot be over-estimated. The orders did not "freeze" workers in their jobs or force employers to keep misfits in their employ. Thousands of applications for transfer were made every month by employers or workers and were agreed to by the National Service Officers. The job controls of the Essential Work Orders merely made it possible to direct the movement of workers according to the needs of the war production program.

With the progress of the war it became necessary to utilise to maximum advantage women workers and men over military age, and also the younger men rejected from the army on medical grounds. These groups were required to register with the Employment Exchanges and were called in for individual interviews. The Exchanges arranged to transfer those who were clearly engaged on unimportant work. Many women were "directed" into gainful work for the first time, and many of them were transferred from home. Many other women who had home ties undertook part-time work. Persuasion and voluntary agreement were used successfully in most cases, but compulsion could be used under the law.

I was always struck by the British genius for persuading people to do voluntarily what their country most needed them to do. Traditional belief in individual liberty was so great that even though compulsory powers existed, they were not used until everything had been done to find a job that the worker would take willingly. The fact that the worker could be ordered to take the job naturally helped him to make up his mind to go of his own volition, but it was important that he felt his decision was his own, and that he knew he was acting within the framework of the trade union program.

Conscription often, of itself, solved marital problems. Where a husband might naturally prefer his wife to stay at home, and where a woman might be torn between carrying out his wishes and a desire to join in and help, conscription stepped in and made the decision for them!

There were no "ceilings" on wages and there was no "freezing" of wages in Great Britain. But a series of measures kept wages within accepted limits. Roughly speaking, by the end of the war, wage rates in industry, including agriculture, had risen by 50 per cent; excluding agriculture, the increase was slightly less. Earnings rose by nearly 80 per cent.

The existence of some elasticity of wage rates helped to make the war economy efficient. The restrictions on the movements of workers could not have been imposed in some industries if wage levels in those industries had been frozen.

It was necessary to raise wages substantially in agriculture and coal-mining and, to some extent, in shipbuilding. Otherwise prevention of workers from leaving occupations in those industries would have caused serious injustice and unrest.

In general, however, demands for wage increases were kept within narrow limits for a long time. This can be attributed to:

(1) The Essential Work Orders, which had the effect of restraining employers from competitive bidding for labor and of keeping workers from "job shopping."

(2) The early imposition of an excess profits tax of 100 per cent. Whatever technical arguments may be advanced against such a high rate, it had a great psychological effect in reconciling the trade unions to a policy of restraint in wage demands. No lower rate would have sufficed for this purpose. To this should be added the unprecedentedly high rate of income tax and other taxes on high income groups.

(3) The maintenance of the cost of living index at a relatively stable level.

(4) The equitable and efficient system of rationing and the price control of food and other basic necessities.

(5) The prohibition of strikes and lockouts with the agreement of organised labor.

(6) The establishment of the tripartite National Arbitration Tribunal with power to make binding decisions.

Each of these closely related measures, before they were put into effect, was fully discussed with the trade unions, who in turn accepted the responsibility of explaining their necessity to the workers. The need to sacrifice traditional rights and accept many forms of compulsion was readily understood by a people who had known Dunkirk and were facing up to the implications of the Battle of Britain.

The importance of holding down prices of basic necessities of everyday consumption can hardly be over-emphasised. Many British workers had wage contracts linked to the cost of living index, but even where there was no formal agreement the importance of stable prices for essentials was of decisive weight in all wage negotiations.

Vigorous measures were taken to deal with prices and supplies of necessities. The methods of price control varied with different commodities. British experience shows, however, that price control of foodstuffs can only be satisfactory when a government purchases supplies and controls the distribution and when the major items of consumer goods are rationed. Sometimes control was first applied at a "bottleneck" through which supplies had to pass between production and consumption stages—for example, the slaughterhouses, the Milk Marketing Board, the flour mills. In some cases control was established by licensing wholesale sellers and distributors. All imports were purchased or taken over by the Government. Home food produce was bought by the Ministry of Food or by a body designated by it. Limits were set, however, on the amounts of some products which the Ministry would buy. This helped to produce an even flow of supplies.

In wartime there is an unavoidable rise in some costs. Therefore, to prevent the price of basic foods from rising, subsidies were used to stabilise the cost to the consumer. This meant that the Government contributed from the general Treasury funds a part of the purchase price of wheat, for example. At the reduced cost wheat was distributed to the miller, who ground it into flour at a fixed charge and distributed it to the baker. This allowed the baker to sell it to the consumer at a low controlled price. This system of subsidising essential articles of food kept the cost of living down. Often the selling price was lower than the buying price for products subsidised.

These products included meat, milk, cheese, butter, bread and potatoes—the least dispensable foods from the nutritional point of view. The subsidies were vital to the health and efficiency of the low income groups, to the government's wage policy and to public morale. The cost of subsidies to the Treasury was saved many times over on total government spendings by the stability introduced into the national economy in lowering living costs to the consumer.

The prices and supplies of clothing and most articles of civilian consumption, other than food, were regulated through the Board of Trade. Thus two departments—the Ministry of Food and the Board of Trade—controlled almost all civilian consumption. Control of supplies, control of prices, and rationing were placed in the same hands. British administrators had little faith in price ceilings with legal penalties for violations, unless at the same time government control was established over supplies and distribution and was administered through the department which controlled the prices.

Food rationing was an outstanding success in the British war economy. On this point there is complete agreement, both by those who have studied it objectively and by those who have lived under it. Methods of rationing were adapted to meet the different conditions of demand and supply of various products and the differing nutritional importance of various foods.

Rationing was also an instrument of general welfare and health policy. The milk ration for an adult was two pints a week, but the Milk Scheme guaranteed to each child under five and to each nursing mother a pint a day and a specified quantity of milk free if the income of the parents was below certain levels. Children and nursing mothers were also given substantial priorities in the distribution of eggs. At that time, the ration was three eggs per month for mothers and three eggs a week for babies—the normal ration being one egg per month per person. Cod-liver oil and orange juice or black-currant juice, or rose-hip syrup, were distributed free for infants. Imported oranges were rationed and reserved wholly for children.

Food was allocated among establishments so as to give larger per capita amounts of some of the most important rationed foods to canteens in factories and workplaces, to "British Restaurants," and to restaurants in working-class districts. "British Restaurants" were communal feeding establishments set up by local authorities with the financial encouragement of the Ministry of Food. They served hot meals for the equivalent of 20 to 25 cents. They were, in fact, government-operated, low-cost cafetarias which proved so satisfactory that some of them have been continued since the war by the local authorities.

Although the low fat ration has told on the nerves and general stamina of the adults, the general health of the children rose during the six years of war. In fact the health of the country was, to the surprise of the medical profession, maintained at a very high level. This is really remarkable when you consider that the week's ration of meat, butter, milk and cheese for one person could easily be eaten in two days, and that the cooking fat allowance for one person a week was about the size of a walnut. Of course there was poultry, but it was scarce and extremely expensive. Fish, though not costly, was often difficult to get owing to shortages due to the danger of mines and enemy attacks on fishing vessels. The rôle of the average housewife can never be sufficiently appreciated. It was her genius and, when that failed, her own ration book that filled the gap and hid the difficulties from her family.

In June 1941 clothes rationing was introduced and, like food rationing, is still in force. About sixty coupons were allowed a year. Articles of clothing could only be obtained by giving up the requisite coupons—twenty-six for a suit, seven for shoes, three for a pair of stockings. Household linen and towels, even handkerchiefs, also came under clothes rationing.

During the war there was no gasoline allowed to owners of private cars except for official use. Heavy casualties in tankers bringing oil and gasoline to the British Isles killed any desire to black market gas or oil. Black marketing in any sphere was practically negligible.

In spite of the compulsory elements in the British system, one was constantly aware that the authorities assumed by the Government were with group consent and had the support of the people. I was deeply moved by Britain's unity of purpose.

There was no greater evidence of this than in the response of the women. They did not start the war with important and interesting jobs. Many were turned away in the early days from some branches of the women's services and civilian defense. They were told that they were too old , or too young, or too inexperienced. Capable women were unemployed. The jobs women did find were frequently menial and were almost invariably so-called "women's jobs."

Before the war women had played, in proportion, a lesser part in British industry than women in the United States, but as the war went deeper and more men were taken into the services, necessity required that women take over. Some factory managers had never employed women and never wanted to ("and besides," they would say, "we have no space to put washrooms for them") but they had to take women or no one. One foreman after another was surprised by their quickness at learning, by the delicacy of their touch, by their dependability. They became a large part of the factory labor of the country.

The extent to which modern warfare absorbed men in the services of supply was not generally realised. I heard Churchill complain that the Royal Air Force, outside of the factory, required seventy men on the ground to keep a plane in the air. In Great Britain alone, signalling, the radio director finder service and collateral observer corps employed the equivalent of two divisions. It was because of the acute shortage of men that the women's auxiliary services of the Navy, Army and Air Force were incorporated at an early period as an integral part of the armed forces of the nation. In a conversation at which I was present, the Prime Minister, while talking with the chief of the anti-aircraft services, criticised the number of soldiers assigned per gun. Discussion ended in a compromise agreement in which the General accepted a reduction of the number of men assigned to him by 40 per cent, with the understanding that his service would be reinforced by the necessary number of women to do the work of the displaced men. Mary Churchill, the Prime Minister's youngest daughter, was present while we were talking. She was only eighteen then. She immediately volunteered for the A.T.S. (army women), enlisting as a private, and was assigned to an anti-aircraft battery. She worked her way through the ranks to a junior commander, which would correspond to a captain in the

United States Army. She was first stationed at a gun site in Hyde Park, and at nights when bombing was heavy it was hard to keep her father away from the area. Later her unit was moved to the South Coast of England to shoot down flying bombs. In the last year of the war she was in command of her company on the Western Front. For these services she was awarded in her own right the M.B.E. (Military Division) for distinguished and gallant conduct.

In December 1941, single women between 20 and 30 were liable for conscription to the forces just as men were, and later the age limit was lowered to include girls of nineteen. But every able-bodied woman between the ages of 18 and 55 was registered for employment and could be directed to labor. The only women who were exempt from war work were those who took care of their children themselves, or had other specially heavy household responsibilities. If they had to keep house for others they were directed to do part-time instead of full-time work.

The organisation of women in the home was an enormous undertaking, and much of its success was due to the untiring effort and understanding of Lady Reading, founder and head of the W.V.S. (Women's Voluntary Service). Women who had only a few hours a day to give were a problem, but the W.V.S. trained some 750,000 of these housewives to be self-reliant and skilled workers of inestimable value to a nation desperately in need of them.

It was not long before the men began to realise the capabilities of the women they had recruited. While large numbers of women everywhere were making first-class jobs of the recognised women's occupations, such as nursing, or being sick orderlies, mess orderlies, clerks, cooks, drivers and stenographers, many did work no one had thought of their doing before.

In the school of army experiments, women with scientific degrees worked on the development of secret devices. A.T.S. at the joint men and women anti-aircraft batteries operated the delicate precision instruments which located raiding planes, and controlled and timed the firing of anti-aircraft guns. A.T.S. also took and developed photographs of shell bursts and calculated mathematically the accuracy of gunnery.

W.A.A.F.s (Air Force women) helped to prepare information from photographs taken before and after bombing raids and military and naval operations. W.A.A.F. meteorologists provided weather forecasts. In the station workshops W.A.A.F.s cleaned and checked and prepared the aircraft while others packed the parachutes or drove the bomb tractors.

W.R.N.S. (Navy women) helped to service and maintain light coastal shipping, and manned many of the small craft of the harbors and waterways. They painted, washed, greased, oiled, took down and serviced engines, serviced the guns, and handled the ammunition. They were electric welders, carpenters, blacksmiths, moulders and pressure gauge testers. W.R.N.S. torpedo women were responsible for the maintenance and adjustment of the torpedoes and for electrical repairs.

As for the Women's Land Army, which numbered over 80,000, there was no type of agricultural work some member did not do—threshing, thatching, tractor ploughing, ditching, caring for stock—everything.

In Southern England this was not always the peaceful occupation that agriculture suggests. The Battle of Britain was fought above their heads, there were constant hit-and-run raids from the French coast and later the droning flying bomb. The most familiar harvesting hymn became, as one of them said, also the most appropriate, for the first line runs:

"We plough the fields and scatter."

Then there were the women ferry pilots, who had to be equally skilled in piloting single or 4-engined planes from factory to airfield. It was not just the occasional woman who was operating a machine or scrubbing a floor. It wasn't a question of *some* women—it was *all* the women. And it wasn't just the women who were used to hard work, but those who formerly lived lives of comparative leisure. Much was required of them in this war—young and old.

In two instances they actively engaged the enemy: the A.T.S. women of the mixed anti-aircraft batteries, and twelve women who were chosen from volunteers to be trained in all the intricate art of espionage and who were dropped by parachute into France when the long-awaited onslaught against imprisoned Europe began. Eight of these women returned, and slipped back quietly and unobtrusively into normal life. Four were captured by the Germans, and drugged and burned in the ovens of Wuppertal Camp.

This deed, and the other atrocities that were committed in concentration camps, make one despair that there is any real progress in the conduct of man. The heart would fail many times were it not that out of the worst that mankind can do the spirit of sacrifice somehow never dies, and the persistent, dogged courage of the human race continues to rise above its crimes, misfortunes and follies.

I have devoted these last pages to the women of Britain for

two reasons. Firstly, because of their undeniable contribution to their country's war effort, but mostly because I believe that it is in the position that women hold in a country, and the attitude of their men towards them, that one can see the advancement or the backwardness of that country's progress. It is because of feeling this I could not be forgetful of the women of my own country. I remembered in the First World War what the long and stern separation from loved ones had meant, and the self-imposed restrictions which they then accepted to support those of us fighting in France. No one would want that again for them. But I knew that if war were forced on us, all that was asked of them would be done.

Nor could any of us be unmindful of the women in resistance movements in occupied countries, who supported their men in the risks they took regardless of their personal safety or that of their families, and who with calm faces and cool nerves hid escaping Allied soldiers and airmen in attics and cellars, knowing well that to be caught meant certain death.

In a superficial sense, I suppose these British women I have described were not what is traditionally thought of as feminine. Certainly not the train woman on the dark platform who roared out directions without a trace of feminine timidity or who heaved heavy trunks for eight hours a day, nor the farm girl whose hand was hard and square and lined, nor the girl pilot, gunner or air-raid warden.

But it was during the time of struggle, out of their homes, away from their husbands and children, that the women of Great Britain cultivated the finest of the latent gifts of all women: an ability to endure and sacrifice.

Each morning during the time of heavy bombing women awoke from a fitful sleep to the miracle of light again, and quiet, and a temporary stopping of danger, and got up and went to work. There was exhilaration then, in spite of fatigue. I like to remember as an accent to this time a story which Lady Reading told me of a woman in Bath who was brought in to a Rest Centre after a raid. She had a black eye and was bruised and shaken but not seriously hurt. She was asked the usual questions, among them whether she was married and, if so, whether her husband was alive. When she replied in the affirmative they said, "Where is your husband?" She looked up at once and said, "In Libya, the bloody coward!"

It has seemed to me of deep significance that the Great Powers which defended the Allied cause all accorded an advanced place to women within their countries and in the war effort, while the nations we fought failed to recognise the dignity of womanhood. The part women played is still a binding force in the light and life of human progress.

XII

THE BATTLE FRONT

In early December 1941 events were moving swiftly to a climax. While battles raged in Europe and in the Middle East, Japan secretly completed her well-laid plans to start an Asiatic war. In order to cover her sinister motives her envoys were negotiating a pact for peace in Washington.

For over two and a quarter years Europe had been torn by the tragedy of war and, for nearly a year of that time, I had watched from Britain the grim struggle for existence.

When I arrived at the beginning of March 1941 the British had withstood a fierce winter at home—dark nights of intense and continuous air attack; days of coping with discomfort, shortages and death. The Germans had failed to invade their island in 1940, but there was no certainty that they would not attempt an invasion in 1941.

British policy was based on the same premise then as in 1940—to hold the enemy while they themselves progressively built up their fighting strength. This last they recognised they could not do without help from the United States.

The only offensive action which could be taken directly from Great Britain was day and night bombing against targets in Germany and German-occupied territories. This form of attack became progressively heavier as production and imports of aircraft increased. In all this we were able to give practical assistance. The import of planes was expedited by the decision to allow American pilots to ferry planes to Great Britain on a commercial basis. This freed R.A.F. pilots from transport duties for military operations. The number of available pilots for the British was also increased when training facilities were opened to them in the United States.

The success of this enforced defensive policy hinged on two vital factors: the security of the British Isles and the maintenance of sea communications.

The defense of the British Isles remained an overriding consideration in their strategy. The war could be won or lost in and around Britain. The only military stroke by which Germany could bring the war to a sudden end would be by a successful invasion. For the British there was no short cut to victory. So long as invasion remained a possibility, forces and equipment needed elsewhere could not be taken away. But even with the enemy only twenty miles from their shores the British took many risks. At no time were their home defenses of sufficient strength. As late as June 1941 total British home defense consisted of three armored divisions, only partially equipped, and twenty-five infantry divisions, which were supplemented by the Home Guard. They had air superiority over their island, thanks to the beating taken by the Germans during the Battle of Britain, but they had to make certain that they kept it.

When one of our Generals visited Great Britain in the summer of 1941 he was allowed to inspect the Channel beach defenses. He was troubled about their inadequacy, and what he felt to be a mistaken concentration of forces on the beaches. He asked that I keep our military authorities informed on coastal Channel defense.

After we were engaged in the war, General Montgomery

was placed at the head of the South-Eastern Command. He asked me to visit him. We met at the Embassy and drove to his headquarters at Reigate. The moment we passed into the area of his command I felt the change of attitude, in discipline and morale. Men everywhere were marching with full packs. It was obvious in watching many of the detachments that they were returning from long route marches. The General saw that I was interested in the condition of the troops and that I had noticed that some of them showed fatigue. He volunteered the information that he wanted his men in training to face all the hardships of actual campaigning. This he felt was insurance for them when they had to face battle conditions.

Even driving down with him I could see the detail of his control and exacting preparation. There was a rapid-fire gun bracketed just across from our seat. Most generals I had travelled with went unarmed. There was a large-faced clock in the back of the driver's seat inside the rear carriage. I wondered what its use might be until I saw the General timing the trucks and other military cars we passed to see if they were keeping inside his speed directive.

He had two outriders. The teamwork between them and the driver was the most perfect I have ever seen. I commented on it. The General told me these three men had been with him when he was on the Continent before Dunkirk. They were plainly devoted to him. When we reached his headquarters there was a smartness which had not always been apparent on similar tours I had made. And yet the spirit of his headquarters' mess was cheery and easy and the men spoke up to him with unusual frankness.

We had hardly arrived when he asked me to join him in climbing a hillside in order to get a view of the terrain, and I guessed also that he did not want to miss his exercise that day. He explained to me that all the officers took long treks each day, many of them, as I found next morning, before breakfast. Everyone was fit and alert. As we moved about the immediate command before dinner he showed me his intercommunication service.

After dinner he took me into his map room and explained to me his entire defense strategy. There were three beaches within his immediate command which might be considered danger areas. These had been heavily mined, and barbed wire and heavy cement obstacles placed along their length. He had taken the men away from the beaches and concentrated them at two strategic road intersections some miles behind the shore line. He had greatly strengthened the three high points that commanded Dover and Folkestone harbors, because he knew that if you denied the Germans the harbors, they could not long sustain a landing force from the beaches.

The next day we inspected all his centres of concentration and also the delicate radar listening posts which could not only pick up the movement of enemy vessels but were also used in directing heavy gunfire. He had reconstituted the relationship between the air and land forces and was himself thinking not only in terms of defense but also of offense. I could see that the whole of his life was absorbed in soldiering, that he was single-purposed and that he had steel in him. He had not asked his men to do what he did not require of his officers.

I reported to General Marshall that I thought he was the best troop commander that I had met in the British military areas.

Second only to the security of her shores was the security of Britain's sea communications. The Home Fleet had to be so disposed as to give maximum protection to supply ships without leaving the South and East Coasts uncovered in the event of invasion. Most of the light ships engaged in protecting the Merchant Marine could be concentrated in the invasion area in five to six days. If these craft had to be diverted from this assignment, and convoying stopped, it would have taken some eight weeks to get the convoys started again. A risk had to be taken; the British could not afford to withdraw this protection until the Germans had actually launched an invasion, for their very existence and power to continue the struggle depended on the Atlantic supply lines.

In the South Atlantic and through the Indian Ocean to the Far East lay her other arteries of communication. Here, the chief problem was again lack of sufficient naval forces for escort duties and hunting groups. The Royal Navy was stretched to the limit in the North Atlantic and in the Mediterranean. In the South Atlantic area, two potential threats existed which had to be carefully watched: (1) if the Germans moved into Spain, Gibraltar would cease to be available as a naval base, with the only alternative the occupation of the Canary Islands and of the Azores. These were commitments for which the British were prepared. The latter move would mean the implementation of the Anglo-Portuguese defensive alliance which had been in existence for several centuries. (2) The increasing danger of Vichy French cooperation with Germany. If the Germans were in Casablanca and Dakar, sea communications in this area would be seriously threatened. Even before the war broke out in Europe, I had talked at great length with the President with regard to Dakar and had taken the trouble to fly down the Mediterranean as well as along the west coast of Africa. It had seemed to me that these would be areas of major importance in the general strategy of a world conflict. Negotiations to keep Vichy France in line were a continuing preoccupation of British and American diplomacy at this time. Relations between the Pétain Government and Britain had been severed as a result of the British bombardment of the French Fleet at Oran the year before. In order to hold the French position against German pressures, I had suggested to the President that he appoint General Pershing as the United States representative to Vichy France. I knew of Pétain's great respect for the Commander-in-Chief of the American Expeditionary Forces in the First World War. General Pershing, as always, was willing to make any sacrifice in the interests of his country. His doctors, however, reported that he was not physically able to accept this assignment. The President, recognising that the French Fleet was a major factor in the balance of sea power, called Admiral Leahy from retirement and asked him to accept this difficult post. The tenacity with which Admiral Leahy conducted a rearguard action in maintaining diplomatic relations in a war-torn Europe has not always been understood or appreciated. He held, for a long period of time, the last outpost in the battle area. No one appreciated more than the British Chiefs of Staff and the Prime Minister himself the value of keeping open this window within the area of German occupation.

I have always thought that Secretary Hull was more than justified in his anger at what he felt was criticism emanating from British official sources, which charged the State Department with collaboration and appeasement because we maintained representation in Vichy. The greatest beneficiaries of this action were the British.

I realised from the beginning, however, the inevitability of the attack on Vichy by General de Gaulle and the Free French. The unconquerable patriots of France had either left the country to join with other armies to fight the enemy or were in underground movements. They together were the backbone of the Free French resistance against Germany. De Gaulle and his Free Frenchmen refused to recognise either the armistice or the surrender. They had no choice but to make war on the Vichy Government. I personally was always in support of the Free French Movement, but I believed that, in the interests of British resistance, the President and Secretary Hull were right in maintaining diplomatic relations in Vichy. It was only natural, however, that this apparent conflict in ideologies was disturbing to many people. They felt that we were compromising our support of the Free French. The situation justified an honest difference of opinion as to where compromise with military necessity should end and action on a basic principle be supported.

It was decided by the Administration that political relations with the Free French would be conducted in Washington, although, on my recommendation, the United States military authorities in London were directed to maintain military liaison with General de Gaulle in London.

There were two issues in this early period in which I took part. The first was to get food to the children in Unoccupied France through the British blockade, and the other was to make certain that the French battleship *Dunkerque* would not fall into enemy hands. We were successful in both. The British made concessions to our request to allow the necessary food-stuffs to pass through the blockade. The French conceded to the President's wishes not to move the *Dunkerque* from Oran to Toulon, and the Prime Minister wrote to the President congratulating him on the success of his intervention with the Vichy Government.

The winter of 1940–41 was one of heavy, unremitting attack by the enemy at sea. It was a nagging, persistent worry affecting the overall picture of the war and a fight to the finish between the hunter and the hunted. Though the people of Britain sensed the danger, they never really knew their perilous position between June 1940 and August 1941. There were attacks by surface craft and aircraft, and increasingly deadly submarines. Then there were the magnetic and acoustic mines. As each new method of attack was launched by the enemy, the losses rose alarmingly.

The surface attacks were dealt with by improving the system of convoying, changes of course, secret effective zig-zagging, all of which lengthened the already over-long journey across the grey Atlantic. But the hunted could turn its vast greyness to good account and convoy after convoy slipped through its mists to port, though not without severe losses.

The underwater menaces were matched by the scientists, who dealt with each new cunning invention with counter inventions of equal cunning and with equal rapidity. The answer to the magnetic and acoustic mines was found in a few short weeks. And always there was the British radar on sea or in the air, that warned the sailor and the airman of the proximity and whereabouts of the enemy, and which turned him in the end from the hunted to the hunter.

And yet for all that could be done, the losses at sea continued to mount dangerously in the early months of 1941.

The real answer was not in defense alone. It had to do with replacements. I had known intimately of the great contribution made by Ray Stevens, George Rublee and Dwight Morrow to Allied shipping control in the First World War, and their high regard for Sir Arthur Salter, who then served as Secretary of the Allied Maritime Transport Council and Chairman of the Allied Maritime Transport Executive. In 1937 Salter had been elected as Independent Member of Parliament for Oxford University. I suggested to the Prime Minister that he send him to Washington to explain British shipping requirements. He proved a tenacious and able representative.

In the first 18 months of the war 7 million tons deadweight of shipping under British control had been lost, and the loss rate had risen to over $7\frac{1}{2}$ million tons a year. Against this, new British building was producing $1\frac{1}{2}$ million tons; the net loss was therefore at the annual rate of 6 million tons, or about a quarter of the entire merchant fleet each year. Besides these crippling losses, there had been, between July 1940 and February 1941 an average of 1,600,000 gross tonnage of shipping laid up for repair.

The opening of the United States shipping yards, arranged under Lend Lease, to permit repair of Allied shipping, helped this critical situation, and for some time aid had been obtained by the addition of ships from occupied countries that had escaped the enemy's control, and by the purchase of some old American ships left over from the earlier war. There was nothing more, however, to be hoped for from these sources. The remaining British tonnage was depleted by the necessity for withdrawing ships for direct military and naval service (for use as armed merchant cruisers and the carriage of troops and their supplies to Egypt, India and other theaters). Under these conditions the imports into the United Kingdom of food and raw materials had fallen to just over half of the pre-war volume, and the prospect ahead was of a much greater

reduction. Starvation and the stoppage of the munitions factories for want of raw materials were an imminent menace. The
position of the oil supplies, conveyed in tankers, on which the
fleet, the air service and the tanks and motor transport of the
armies all depended, was equally desperate.

There was no possible means of salvation except from the
United States. But the American merchant fleet was com-
paratively small and was fully engaged in the pursuits of
maritime commerce. American shipbuilding was also on a
small scale; it had almost ceased for the greater part of the
inter-war period and was then producing only one million
tons a year.

The immediate emergency was met by an order from
President Roosevelt to divert two million tons of shipping to
the war service. This order was successfully executed by
bringing into use the enemy and neutral tonnage which had
been immobilised in United States ports, and by transferring
to rail the traffic between the West and East Coasts which had
previously been carried through the Panama Canal by our
ships, thus releasing a certain tonnage ordinarily engaged in
intercoastal trade.

On April 9th, President Roosevelt concluded an agreement
with the Danish Minister in Washington whereby the United
States undertook the defense of Greenland.

On April 11th, President Roosevelt declared the Red Sea
no longer a combat zone and, from then on, American
materials were carried in American ships to any port in the
Middle East area.

At midnight on April 24th, aircraft and warships of the
United States received orders to patrol convoy routes over a
very considerable part of the Atlantic, and to shadow raiders

and U-boats and to broadcast their position in plain language to the world, at four-hour intervals.

On July 7th, the President announced that American forces had landed in Iceland, and would take over its defense. From this time onward, American naval forces escorted British convoys as far as Iceland, though the other reaches of the North Atlantic had to remain a combat zone from which ships flying the United States flag were excluded until November 1941.

But the final answer depended upon the extent to which American shipbuilding could be rapidly increased. Sir Arthur Salter, then in Washington, had made calculations which indicated that, for the European war, a shipbuilding program in the amount of eight million tons, or some 800 Liberty ships, was imperative during the year 1942. This appeared to be an enormous undertaking. At a meeting attended by President Roosevelt, Harry Hopkins, Sir Arthur Salter, Admiral Land and Admiral Vickery, the President endorsed Sir Arthur's estimate and directed that the ships be built.

It was Sir Arthur Salter who presented the facts in the case. Admiral Vickery was given the responsibility of carrying out the building program.

It was a stupendous task. The plans were completed by the end of 1941; the program was completed by the end of 1942. The extent of accomplishment was unequalled and unapproached in history. Great as this victory was, it proved only a temporary relief. The brighter prospect—so dearly won, was rudely shattered by coming events. Pearl Harbor, which plunged the United States into war, not only enlarged the scope of operations, but augmented the rate of losses to a scale never before experienced. Once again the seemingly impossible had to be achieved. The American shipbuilding program of 800 Liberty ships a year was later raised to some 20 million tons or 2,000 Liberty ships a year, in order to satisfy the voracious demands of the many theaters of war on every continent and all of the seven seas.

But all this comes later on in the story. For the moment the small group of men who did the planning and the execution for the Government at the President's directive, the earlier arrangement of the British with Henry Kaiser to build a new type of standard ship, the men who managed and manned the shipyards, had turned the hour-glass back. The prospects on the eve of Pearl Harbor, against all earlier expectations, were that shipbuilding in the United States would replace losses as they were then running, and would meet the demands of the European War by the end of the following year.

In the fall of 1941, Mr. Churchill was able to announce to the House of Commons that there had been an easement in the Battle of the Atlantic, and that, whereas in the four months ending June, shipping losses had been at the rate of 500,000 tons a month, in the four months ending October they had fallen to an average of 180,000 tons a month. During the same period the enemy mercantile marine was being crushed out of existence.

One of the outstanding battles of 1941, and certainly of naval warfare, was the chase and sinking of the great German battleship *Bismarck*.

In May the *Bismarck* and the *Prinz Eugen* were discovered by British air reconnaissance sheltering in the Norwegian port of Bergen. It was thought that they would try to make an attack on British convoys coming from the United States. Two days later, on Friday, May 23rd, they were seen by British cruisers passing through the straits between Iceland and Greenland, and they were engaged by the *Prince of Wales* and the *Hood*. The following day Mr. Churchill told me that he had had news that the *Hood* had been sunk in the engagement and that probably all aboard had been lost. On the Sunday the Admiralty informed me that the *Bismarck* had been hit by a torpedo, but because of bad weather she had gotten away under cover of darkness. I got no more news of this sea battle until Monday, when the Prime Minister asked me to join him in the Map Room at the Admiralty. The *Bismarck* had been again sighted by a Catalina aircraft. When this was known Mr. Churchill said in his report to the Commons "the whole apparatus of our ocean control came into play." This was centred in the Map Room. I had never seen the battle techniques of modern naval warfare until that day. The controls reached out to every port, to every vessel, across the vast oceans, with radar communications to airports and planes, all pinpricked on a single point of attack. Two things that impressed me as soon as I came into the room were the quietness and efficiency of the place. Except for Mr. Churchill and the First Lord of the Admiralty, I was the only civilian there. There were many naval officers who stood talking in low voices among themselves. Flashbacks were coming in from everywhere. It took very little imagination to see the *Bismarck*, alone, without her escort, wounded and under attack from Fleet Air Arm planes. We were surrounded by maps that covered all the walls. Every ship afloat in every sea was marked out on them. Admiral Sir Dudley Pound, the First Sea Lord, had complete command of the situation. He was one of Britain's greatest naval Chiefs of Staff. All outgoing and incoming messages were handed to him, and on receiving them he at once passed them on to the Prime Minister, who insisted that I see every message. Churchill was a familiar figure in this inner sanctum of the Royal Navy. It was he who had mobilised the Fleet before the last war and had again taken command as First Lord of the Admiralty in the early days of this war. There was no detail of the interchange that was not familiar to him. We stayed there the entire afternoon, and then drove back to the Annex. He went on to the Commons and I returned to the Embassy. The next day I went to Parliament to hear his report of the progress of this naval engagement. He explained that during the night four more torpedoes had hit the *Bismarck* and that she was helplessly circling in the open sea under attack by British warships. He ended his remarks by the brief statement that, in a few days, it would be possible to give a much more detailed account of this engagement with the most powerful battleship afloat, and that there was every reason to be satisfied with the outcome of this fierce and memorable naval encounter. A short time after Mr. Churchill had taken his seat, a messenger handed him a note. He rose from his place and interrupted the debate to say "I do not know whether I might venture, with great respect, to intervene for one moment. I have just received news that the *Bismarck* is sunk." The House broke into pandemonium. It was difficult to continue the debate.

Through all these trials Eire remained adamantly neutral. There had been a period of great tension between Britain and Eire late in 1940 over the naval bases on the west coast of Ireland which Britain had given up in 1938. If the British Navy had been able to use these bases with air support, the war against the U-boats could have been pressed more aggressively and many British lives and cargoes would have been saved. But de Valera realised this would have opened Eire to air bombardment by the Germans, and he refused to turn back the bases. In the spring of 1941 a new crisis was threatening to arise in the relations between the two countries. There was a move on the part of the government of Northern Ireland to enforce conscription in that area. Mr. Churchill was impressed by the arguments in support of such a program. He felt that, since conscription was rigorously imposed on the rest of the United Kingdom, there should be equal sacrifice everywhere. The Chamberlain agreement of 1938, however, had included a promise to withhold such action even in time of war. I personally felt that little advantage would be gained by unilaterally breaking this agreement. Policing the border between Northern Ireland and Eire could have absorbed as many men as the conscription in Northern Ireland would have added to the armed forces. It was the opinion of the Prime Minister of Australia, Mr. R. G. Menzies, who was in London at the time, that this measure would be adversely received in his Commonwealth, where a quarter of the population is of Irish Catholic origin. I felt that this measure would stir up old resentments in the United States. I also knew that large numbers of citizens from Eire were volunteers in the British Army, and almost half a million were working on the farms and in the factories in England and Scotland. I cabled the facts to the President. He replied at once saying he hoped no action would be taken. I took the matter up with the Prime Minister. We discussed the issue for several hours. He did not carry out the recommendation made by the Government of Northern Ireland.

I have always liked the Irish, but did not pretend to understand the position of Eire in the war. There is a nice story of a boy from the South of Ireland who was a volunteer gunner in the Royal Air Force. His plane was one of many engaged in a raid over Berlin. They had run into heavy anti-aircraft fire.

Flares and flak were bursting all around them, when he turned to another member of the crew and said, "Thank God 'Dev' has kept us out of all this!"

In this year of 1941 the Germans had a total of two hundred and fifty divisions in the field. They were powerful enough to fight the Russians in the East, and they maintained forces in Western Europe which the British could not tackle single-handed. This limited British strategy to the destruction of the foundations upon which the German war machine was built— by blockade to strangle its economy; by bombing to destroy its factories and transport, and unsettle its morale; by subversive activities and propaganda to encourage and sustain resistance in occupied countries and to win the support of neutrals; but, meanwhile, to build up slowly but surely the forces and accumulate the stores of material needed for an eventual return to the Continent.

After Germany attacked Russia in June, the first flush of their success carried them by October to the gates of Leningrad in the north, Moscow in the centre, and Rostov in the south. Here they met a stone wall of resistance. The mammoth struggle was watched with the greatest anxiety. The "military planners" of the West prepared alternative plans, and the whole future strategy of the war hung in the balance.

Immediately after the struggle on the Eastern front began, offers of assistance and exchange of military missions between Great Britain and Russia took place. The visit by Harry Hopkins to Moscow in August had resulted in a joint message from President Roosevelt and the Prime Minister to Marshal Stalin promising provision of the maximum possible supplies required by Russia. In September the Anglo-American Supply Mission made practical arrangements to carry through these promises. This resulted in the United States and Great Britain undertaking to send vast quantities of war material, particularly aircraft, anti-aircraft guns, tanks and anti-tank guns (perhaps the most precious commodities of all) to Russia.

Small convoys to north Russia began in August 1941. It was at the same time that the British agreed to transfer to them 200 Curtiss Tomahawk fighters, which had reached England and could be quickly despatched to Archangel. We had, however, to provide the necessary spare parts, ground equipment and ammunition. The Russians had never seen this type of plane, so the British sent on four mechanics experienced in erecting and servicing them, and I assigned two officers from the Embassy who had been flying them. They told me on their return that, with this small force to assist them, the Russians had assembled the planes in an incredibly short time and the pilots flew them without difficulty.

Another side of the picture which is easily forgotten, but which is directly related to future operations, was the failure of Raschid Ali's revolt in Iraq, and the entry of the British troops into Iran in August 1941. The main object of this advance was to ensure a supply line to Russia. Its later importance in channelling Lend Lease aid to the Eastern Front would be hard to exaggerate.

The cardinal point of German strategy in 1942, if Rommel had successfully penetrated into Egypt, was to capture Cairo and thrust north-east to join the other arm of the German pincers moving east toward Russia. The occupation of Iran also formed a last line of defense against this threat. Rommel was stopped at El Alamein, but that is a later story.

By the end of November, the German advance in Russia had slowed down. In other words, a forced stabilisation on most of the Russian front had taken place. Bad communications, maintenance difficulties, lack of reserves and exposure of their troops to winter weather, on the one hand, and, on the other, the determined and courageous resistance of the Russians, had turned the tide. An invasion of the British Isles was a receding danger; in the Middle East, where the British had feared a German advance through the Caucasus to the Caspian and the Baku oilfields, the Russians now gave complete protection to their western flank, enabling the British to withdraw forces from the Levant-Caspian front for the Far East.

The Middle East was the only theater in which Britain was able to engage the enemy on land. The swift success of British forces against the Italian armies in Cyrenaica had gone far toward accomplishing the first objective in this theater—the elimination of Italy. By February 1941 General Wavell's Desert Army was on the border of Tripolitania, and, for the time being—but not for long—the enemy was cleared from the Western Desert. In East Africa, the British had captured Abyssinia, Eritrea, Italian Somaliland and reclaimed British Somaliland. The Italian Fleet had suffered defeat off Cape Matapan.

The Germans, however, were progressively active in the Middle East theater at this time. Hungary, Rumania and Bulgaria had been occupied, and, with Yugoslavia a virtual prisoner, there were indications of an invasion of Greece or Turkey. From air bases in Sicily, German bombers began their attacks on Malta in January. From Tripolitania, they were able to bomb British troops in Benghazi.

"The movement of the German air forces and armored troops from Italy and Sicily into Tripoli had begun even before we took Benghazi, and our submarines and aircraft have taken a steady toll of the transports carrying German troops and vehicles. But that has not prevented—and could not prevent—their building up a strong armored force on the African shore." So said Mr. Churchill in a speech to the House of Commons on April 9th. In the last week in March the Germans began an advance in strength from Tripolitania. Weakened by their commitments elsewhere, British forces, by April 17th, were back at the Egyptian frontier. Tobruk alone remained—an isolated fortress enabling the British to threaten the enemy's lines of communication along the coast roads.

Greece and Yugoslavia were attacked by Germany early in April. I have already told the story of British aid in this area. It was insufficient, and by April 30th British forces had been evacuated from Greece, after heavy losses. By the end of June, Crete had fallen and German forces were in occupation of the Dodecanese.

In Syria, the widespread infiltration of Germans had reached proportions which made it necessary for a large force of British and Free French troops to invade the country in June. By July 11th, the Germans had been driven out and the conquest of Syria was complete.

The results of these two operations put the Allies into a far better position at the eastern end of the Mediterranean. Naval and air control became effective and direct contact was obtained with Turkey.

Throughout the year conditions in Malta gave cause for much anxiety. This island was the strategic British naval base in the Mediterranean. Bombing attacks from Italian bases were continuous. The need for fighter aircraft reinforcements was urgent. These were delivered by aircraft carrier through the Mediterranean.

The neutrality of Spain and of Turkey was of constant importance to the Allies, though the participation of the latter in the war would have been clearly to their own advantage.

There are no better words than Mr. Churchill's to sum up the battle position in the Middle East in the early fall of 1941:

"If we now look back for a moment, we can measure the solid improvement in our position in the Middle East or East which has been achieved since the French suddenly fell out of the war and the Italians made haste so eagerly to come in against us. At that date all we had in those parts was from 80,000 to 100,000 men, starved of munitions and equipment, which had all been sent to the French front, always first to claim the best we had. We had lost our means of safe communication through the Mediterranean and almost all the main bases on which we relied. We were anxiously concerned for our defense of Nairobi, Khartoum, British Somaliland, and, above all, of the Nile Valley and Palestine, including the famous cities of Cairo and Jerusalem. None was safe; but, nevertheless, after little more than a year we have managed to gather very large and well-equipped armies, which already begin to approach 750,000, which possess and are being supplied with masses of equipment of all kinds. We have developed an air force almost as large as that we had in Great Britain when the war began, an air force which is rapidly expanding. We have conquered the whole of the Italian Empire in Abyssinia and Eritrea, and have killed or taken prisoner the Italian armies of over 400,000 men by which these regions were defended. We have defended the frontiers of Egypt against German and Italian attack. We have consolidated our position in Palestine and Iraq. We have taken effective control of Syria and provided for the security of Cyprus. Finally, by the swift, vigorous campaign in Persia which has taken place since the House (of Commons) last met, we have joined hands with our Russian allies, and stand in the line to bar the further eastward progress of the enemy."

One more event took place in the Middle East in the period immediately preceding the attack on the United States, and that was the offensive launched by British forces in the Western Desert on November 19th. The fortress of Tobruk was relieved on November 27th and British forces began their second advance westward.

Throughout the whole period, the attitude of Japan had to be carefully watched. The possibility of Japanese aggression was never far off and there were many uneasy moments before the final treachery of December 7th.

It was a cardinal feature of British policy—and this policy was supported by United States military opinion—that all efforts must be concentrated on the war against Germany and Italy and only the minimum necessary for defense reserved against the possibility of a felon blow from Japan. Thus, the British garrisons in the Far East—at Singapore, Hong Kong, in Burma, Malaya—were but a fraction of what was needed. In Burma, the equivalent of two divisions was made up of Indian and Burmese troops; in Malaya, three and a half to four divisions of Australian, Indian and Malayan troops; at Hong Kong little more than two infantry brigades and the local volunteer force.

Since it was felt that security would depend primarily on air power, efforts were made to build up the air forces, but the aircraft were negligible in quantity and obsolete in type.

The Royal Navy could not afford to send sufficient units to form a line of battle against the Japanese Navy, though the help given by the United States in the Battle of the Atlantic enabled the battleship *Prince of Wales* and the battle cruiser *Repulse* to be sent to Far Eastern waters in November. It was hoped that these ships might play the part of "rogue elephants," and that they would keep the Japanese guessing.

This is roughly the story of the battle fronts and the disposition of the British forces in the early days of December 1941.

XIII

PEARL HARBOR

As 1941 drew to its close, I began to realise that the peace negotiations with Japan then being carried on in Washington might not be successful.

On November 30th I forwarded to the President a message from Mr. Churchill, in which the Prime Minister suggested that there was still an untried avenue of approach in averting war between Japan and "our two countries," namely, a plain declaration that any further act of aggression by Japan would lead to the gravest consequences.

Churchill said he realised the Constitutional difficulties that confronted the President in taking such action, and begged him to consider whether, at the correct moment, which might be very near, the President would say that any further Japanese aggression would compel him to place the issue before the Congress of the United States.

Mr. Churchill went on to state that his country would make a similar declaration, and, in any case, arrangements were being made to synchronise "our action with yours." Whether such a communication should be secret or public, the exact timing of such a message, and whether it be done jointly or simultaneously by each country, he left to the judgment of the President.

I was later able to get consent from the British Government for the release of this message for the use of the Congressional

Committee investigating the facts surrounding the surprise attack on Pearl Harbor.

Most of the information that reached us at the Embassy was through British channels. Their concern was as great as our own. The tenseness at the Embassy was felt in Whitehall.

It had been arranged that I should go down to Eden's house in the country on Friday evening, December 5th. He was to leave for Moscow on Sunday morning, taking with him a memorandum for Marshal Stalin which he hoped might be the basis of a joint statement on war aims and plans for post-war organisation of peace. This conformed with the fundamental principles of the Atlantic Charter to which the Russians had agreed at the Inter-Allied Conference on September 24th. Mr. Eden had shown this memorandum to me in its original form in order to get a judgment on the reactions in the United States. Since then the Cabinet had made certain changes which he wanted me to know about.

It was an important engagement, but it was in my mind that the Japanese were on the prowl, and General Chaney and Admiral Ghormley were out of London on work jobs connected with liaison with the British High Command. So I postponed leaving London, and on Saturday morning I picked up through British intelligence sources the fact that two Japanese convoys, one of 25 transports, 6 cruisers and 10 destroyers, and the other of 10 transports, 2 cruisers and 10 destroyers, had been sighted off Cambodia Point moving slowly westward towards Kra. I telegraphed this at once to the State Department.

I did not reach Eden's house until Saturday shortly before midnight. He found me some supper and we stayed up until the early hours of the morning discussing his mission to Moscow. We both had great faith in the Russians as fighting allies and equal belief in their ultimate desire for a peaceful world.

The next morning Eden left at 10 o'clock. He urged me to stay and get some rest as Mrs. Eden and her brother were both staying on. I told him no, that I wanted to go to Chequers to see the Prime Minister, that I thought the Japanese were on the road to war. Whom, when and where they were going to attack I said I did not know; but that I thought it would be soon, and wanted to be with Churchill. Eden was sorry to be going out of the country at that moment because he also felt that Great Britain, at least, was in for trouble.

When I reached Chequers, a hundred miles away, the Prime Minister was walking up and down outside the entrance door —the others had gone in to lunch twenty minutes before. He asked me if I thought there was going to be war with Japan. I answered "Yes." With unusual vehemence he turned to me and said:

"If they declare war on you, we shall declare war on them within the hour."

"I understand, Prime Minister. You have stated that publicly."

"If they declare war on us, will you declare war on them?"

"I can't answer that, Prime Minister. Only the Congress has the right to declare war under the United States Constitution."

He did not say anything for a minute, but I knew what was in his mind. He must have realised that if Japan attacked Siam or British territory it would force Great Britain into an Asiatic war, and leave us out of the war. He knew in that moment that his country might be "hanging on one turn of pitch and toss."

Nevertheless he turned to me with the charm of manner

that I saw so often in difficult moments, and said, "We're late, you know. You get washed and we will go in to lunch together."

Most of the guests left early, and those of us who were staying spent a quiet afternoon. Averell Harriman and Kathie, his daughter, went for a walk with me. The Prime Minister worked for a time and then rested, as he had been up most of the night before. Mrs. Churchill was not well and did not come down to dinner.

These are simple incidents, unremarkable as any day's happenings until some terrible or dramatic event imprints them on one's mind forever.

It was a few minutes before nine o'clock when we went into the dining-room. The Prime Minister looked very grim and sat in complete silence. It was his custom to listen to the 9 o'clock broadcast which usually gave the fullest summary of the day's news. Just before the hour struck he roused himself and called out to Sawyers, the butler, to put the radio on the table. It was a small fifteen-dollar portable set that Harry Hopkins had sent him after his return to the United States. The Prime Minister reached out his hand and raised the lid that set it going. For a moment there was a jangle of music, and then, suddenly, from the little black box, a voice announced that Japan had attacked our fleet at Pearl Harbor.

Even allowing for the difference in time, it meant that the radio had got the momentous news to the Prime Minister of Great Britain two hours late, but before the intelligence services of either country had been able to inform the British High Command.

We looked at one another incredulously. Then Churchill jumped to his feet and started for the door with the announcement, "We shall declare war on Japan." There is nothing half-hearted or unpositive about Churchill—certainly not when he is on the move. Without ceremony I too left the table and followed him out of the room.

"Good God," I said, "you can't declare war on a radio announcement."

He stopped and looked at me half-seriously, half-quizzically, and then said quietly, "What shall I do?" The question was asked not because he needed me to tell him what to do, but as a courtesy to the representative of the country attacked.

I said, "I will call up the President by telephone and ask him what the facts are."

And he added, "And I shall talk with him too."

We got through to the White House in a few minutes and the President told me very simply the story of the attack—so tragic in itself and yet the final mistake that was to end the power of the Axis. He could not, however, over the open transatlantic telephone, tell the extent of the crashing losses sustained by the fleet, or the heavy casualties. I said I had a friend with me who wanted to speak to him. I said, "You will know who it is, as soon as you hear his voice."

Shortly after we had finished talking with the President, Anthony Eden telephoned from Invergordon, where he was boarding a destroyer for Murmansk, to say he had picked up the flash on Pearl Harbor. The Prime Minister told him that he had already decided to go to Washington himself. Eden asked if he should not postpone his own trip. The Prime Minister said he thought it would be better for him to go on to Moscow as planned. I had a brief talk with Eden. We were all in agreement.

It was later that night that we got the report that the

Japanese had also attacked the British in Malaya. We spent the night in helping the Prime Minister send out messages. The next day Great Britain declared war on Japan. On the afternoon of this same day President Roosevelt approved a joint resolution of Congress declaring a state of war between the United States and Japan. On December 11th, Germany and Italy declared war on the United States.

The days of peace were over for us. The wide waters of the great oceans could not keep the flames of war away from our shores. We, too, had to learn that peace is indivisible and global.